feeling unimportant and ordinary?

unleashed

discover God's
extraordinary journey
for your life

steve oeffling

Unleashed
by Steve Oeffling

Printed in the United States of America

ISBN 978-0-692-31040-3

Produced and packaged by The Michael Thomas Group
www.themichaelthomasgroup.com

table of contents

Comfort
is Overrated

Breathtaking. Incredible. Awesome. Words fail to describe the beauty of Niagara Falls, the most powerful waterfall in North America. This natural wonder forms the border between neighbors, the United States and Canada, and joins the Great Lakes Erie and Ontario. Tourists flock to the area to see this spectacular sight.

To appreciate the grandeur of the Falls, you must begin at Lake Erie just below Buffalo, New York, where the Niagara River begins its seventeen-mile journey. On the river's relatively calm western shore winds a parkway dotted with lovely homes and immaculate lawns. Orchards of fruit trees and grapes debut in a pleasant pastoral setting.

As you continue your journey, the Niagara River looks like many other rivers — wide, deep, but apparently ordinary. This waterway won't seem ordinary for long! For as the river continues, its pace quickens, flowing with increasing energy. In the distance, a mist appears. Then, sound enters the scene — faint at first but quickly building.

You soon realizes what's coming. The faint sound increases in volume to become a thunderous roar as you reach the Falls. Amazing! In some places, the very ground rumbles as this river suddenly drops some 165 feet below. Six million cubic feet of water crash over the edge every minute.

The breathtaking sight calls for lingering, for praise to the One who made it all. The journey takes us beyond ourselves. We're caught up in a special moment when our senses affirm bigness, something greater than us. The journey not only catches our attention; the experience captures our hearts. Other sounds vanish with the mist as we're overcome with the majesty of God. We sense a oneness in what He's doing, yet what I've described is only part of the story.

Our challenge lies in understanding the significance of our lives as part of what God longs to accomplish.

As early as the mid-nineteenth century, people wondered if this majestic scene could also bring a practical benefit to people. Engineers dug huge underground tunnels to divert over half of the river's water, and by 1881, large electrical generating systems were developed. Not many years later, Buffalo became the first community in North America with streets lit by electrical power.

Today, this mighty river generates enough power to serve millions of homes and businesses. The river is *unleashed.*

My description parallels something even more spectacular and powerful as God's creative hand delivers both beauty and benefit. The parallel is you and me. We may appear ordinary as we flow through our years. Like a river, we encounter a few rocks or eddies as part of the human experience. Some stretches of our lives run with calm predictability; others quicken with the unexpected.

Our challenge lies in understanding the significance of our lives as part of what God longs to accomplish.

Whether you recognize it or not, God is directing your course. Have you ever thought about God's power being unleashed in you?

Journey? What Journey?

As a university student some years ago, I signed up to follow Christ. I meant it, willing to go anywhere, do anything to serve Jesus, at any time. In light of what I knew about God's love for me, that commitment just made sense. This eventually led to a pastoral role in the local church, although this detail isn't the important part of the journey. As time passed, I never looked back with regrets for I loved what the journey brought. I worked hard and enjoyed the company of many others along the way.

Gradually, a vague unsettledness, still difficult to describe, grew within. Ministry progressed well with no major crises apart from the usual challenges we all face. I still loved Jesus and delighted to serve Him, but life had grown routine. I wondered about the significance of my life especially in light of my relationship with Jesus and the more adventurous tone of His Word.

A friend approached me with an invitation to join him on an international trip to share God's good news and establish a new church. I bought my tickets and cleared my schedule. Then I watched my friend back out, leaving me to work in an impoverished slum of a major South American city — alone and not knowing anyone on the team.

Armed with three Spanish words in my vocabulary bag — "Sí," "No," and "Baño — I found myself in a new position — that of need. I struggled to figure out why I needed a two-digit room number which I could never pronounce correctly. My attempts to communicate were hilarious as I held up my sheet of paper with the number 46 on it in order to receive my room key. I lived with people who came to faith out of deep pain from rather dramatic backgrounds in the city's drug alleys and crack houses. Elevated levels of danger were part of my experience, and I occasionally thought, *If this goes badly, no one will even know where to find my body.* Most of the time, I didn't know where I was.

As my predictable, rather comfortable life grew very uncomfortable, I processed these new experiences and realized God was at work. I was deep in the river's whitewater going somewhere still unknown to me; but wherever the journey led, I was certain God had the details covered. Strangely, I loved this new world.

I was learning comfort was overrated. God's plan for me transcended personal prosperity.

The journey transported me into various cultures to meet people and churches previously outside my experience. A new circle of friends became part of my life — people whose stories included murder, drugs, and prison, but now were transformed by the gospel. For example, Elsa had multiple lesbian relationships. We visited her former partners to share the news of her new life in Christ, and through her people came to faith in Jesus. The faith I believed and taught burst into life before my eyes. Though challenged, I experienced God's presence in powerful ways. Wherever this was all going it would to be life-changing.

When I returned home, I told the stories of my trip to everyone who would listen and showed pictures whether people were interested or not. My home church was wonderfully gracious, trying to figure out what was going on with their pastor. I attempted to understand it as well. For a period of time, I multi-tasked processing my new experiences along with the responsibilities of my life and work.

Looking back, I can best describe this season as "life-giving." It's not that I especially enjoyed uncomfortable settings; the exhilaration came in seeing what God was doing up close and personal both in and through me. In the Swahili language, Africans have incorporated the Arabic term "safari" to describe journeys or adventures in the face of the unknown. My personal safari commenced.

I felt like I was walking through biblical times, in some ways identifying with Jesus' early followers who witnessed God's power at work through them. I learned something important happens when we leave our protective spheres of comfort.

Something important happens when we leave our protective spheres of comfort.

What I'm describing may sound a bit scary, but in reality, my story doesn't parallel a Stephen King thriller. While there was a sense of adventure, God affirmed me as kingdom work advanced and personal transformation continued. Much like the Niagara River increased in energy on its journey, I was caught up in something God was orchestrating.

What Do You Really Believe?

Abraham and Sarah were my biblical heroes in those days. I loved them. My wife and I identified with how God called them to leave the comfortable and familiar. One evening we looked up into the unobstructed Middle Eastern sky where these biblical people of faith once travelled. Above us stretched a mass of stars, and the reality of the moment hit us.

Four thousand years earlier, Abraham looked up into the sky and saw the same stars. The same God we serve gave him a promise, a promise of His presence on the journey. We sensed the identical promise. Abraham's decision to take the journey would bring blessing to him and his family, and while undoubtedly harder to comprehend, Abraham's journey would somehow result in blessing that would be global in nature.

The journey for Abraham and Sarah had its uncomfortable moments for sure. Camping or extended travel loses its excitement after a short time. I imagined interesting husband-wife dinner conversations around the camp fire. "So tell me again, why are we doing this? Are you sure it was God speaking?" There were new people, new experiences, and new cultures; yet they drove Abraham and Sarah to trust the Lord God as they got to know Him in intimate ways.

But we're getting ahead of ourselves in the story. As I returned from those early border crossings, I was forced to examine what I really believed. Swimming in whitewater that moves at a faster-than-comfortable pace compels a person to see God in fresh ways.

I began a project which I later encouraged our church leaders to participate in. "What are your core beliefs?" I asked them. "Spend time meditating on this." I didn't mean the typical doctrinal statement to which people subscribe. Those formal statements have their place. *I believe Jesus is God and the Savior sent from God. Salvation flows from God's grace through faith. The Bible is God's Word. Eternal life is real.* These truths along with many others remain precious to me. In fact they have grown in certainty.

Instead, I wanted the church leaders to discover the core values that grow out of their beliefs. How do I live in light of what I believe? Does what I profess as a Christ-follower have any meaningful day-to-day implications? How do my beliefs affect the choices I make or the lifestyle I live? Is the use of my abilities or resources affected by my beliefs?

I settled on values which became foundational in life direction and decision-making. Some of my values concerned people, such as the importance of my family and investment in lost people. Others were God-focused as my heart awakened to an incredible sense of wonder that surrounds God and His ways. I felt this in creative displays like Niagara Falls or a star-filled sky; I also saw it in God's creative plans for His people and His world. God is more amazing than I thought. His power is greater than I imagined. His love and grace are deeper than I had known. And His plans are almost beyond understanding.

As I experienced this amazing God, there were major life implications. I wanted to be part of His plans even though I had little idea of what this meant. I just wanted in. Reading about Abraham and Sarah, I figured I was in good company as they appeared clueless about the details of their future as well. They just trusted God who led them.

This value impacted my life in another way. It changed the way I see life and God's heart. I always had a bent toward optimism; now I no longer saw a glass as half full or half empty. I found myself searching for a bigger glass to catch the spillover of what God wanted to do. I really believed this, and it became an operating principle in my life.

A couple of friends once remarked to me, "Steve, how can you stay positive when your day is going poorly?" All I could say was, "There's always a wonder to God's ways." That's simply who He is. When everything is expanding and running on all cylinders, God is amazing. And likewise, when it's all in the tank, then God continues to work even in our disappointment or pain. In fact, God does some of His best work in the dark where we can't see clearly or make sense of life.

Your Journey is Unlike Anyone Else's

So, what does all this talk of God's greatness and plans mean for you? Is it possible to experience a tangible life difference as you participate in the journey God has designed? I'm optimistic regardless of who you are!

For example, think about your abilities. You may have attained great fame and success. Or maybe not. You may not rate yourself in the superstar category when it comes to godliness. You may feel like me in personal struggles with fears or inadequacies or even spiritual gifting. In this book, you'll meet people just like you. They come from various walks of life and from distant parts of the globe with few resources. If you met them on the street, they wouldn't seem to be anything but ordinary, and that's why their stories are so important. In fact, they will challenge how you define ordinary.

My hope is you'll see yourself in this book. It's not a collection of superhero stories; rather it's a look into what a wondrous God can do in any person. I want you to catch a glimpse of God's heart and His plans. You'll see He is awesome — particularly in light of how you fit into His work today. God is transforming the lives of people, some of whom you will read about in this book. Their stories and experiences are real. I have changed names and precise locations of some to protect them as they work in sensitive areas.

While reading this, you may say, "I'm happy for you, but my situation is unique." True enough, but let me put your mind at ease. I'll shy away from giving trite and simple ways to live. You'll not find a list of things you ought to do nor will I give you thirteen easy steps to fulfill God's plans for your life. Frankly, there's nothing easy about the process. I won't ask you to try harder to be a better Christian. Most of us have learned what a black hole that can be.

All of these areas belong in the realm of the Spirit's work in your life. By definition, application is always personal, so I've included a reflective section at each chapter's conclusion. A journey of grace awaits you marked by steps of learning, growth, and joy. Sure, the water can get choppy, but I promise a liberating journey that matters.

Obstacles are normative in the Christian life and no match for the God who desires to unleash His people.

We'll talk about obstacles that hinder us on the journey. Some of them have become such a familiar part of our lives that we may not recognize them for what they are. We may fail to see how they keep God's power from being unleashed in our lives. Other barriers will look new, even as the new territory we travel appears strange, perhaps daunting. But obstacles can be overcome. Obstacles are normative in the Christian life and no match for the God who desires to unleash His people.

Please understand this isn't just my story. My wife and family form a major part of the journey, as they've walked many of the steps with me. My amazing church stretches across this journey. Something powerful occurred in this body of people. Much like the force of the Niagara, God favored our church family with opportunities to bring His Kingdom blessings to people in our community and world. The same opportunities lie before you.

Yet journeys must have a starting point. A willingness to begin is essential. An ancient Chinese proverb reminds us that a journey of a thousand miles begins with a single step. I'll introduce you to wonderful people in this book who pondered those first steps. The quality of their lives will be noted without putting them on pedestals. We'll learn from their stories, as each was willing to believe God would launch them into the journey and have the power to take it from there.

The final group to impact my journey is a team of international partners and leaders who would not want any of the attention attached to them. I see them as the cream of the crop in the kingdom. Most will not fully understand how they have impacted me by their commitment and courage.

As we begin, I offer you an invitation to the journey. I've seen glimpses of God's power unleashed and stood amazed on several occasions to see Niagara-like impact on cultures with its life-giving water and energy. I long to see more — God's people unleashed on grander scales for His glory and for the good of the world that needs Him. God calls us to this aim. So, if you are wondering if this book is for you, may I simply say, "Read on."

"The trouble is that, as modern people, we have too much to live with and too little to live for ... Deep in our hearts, we all want to find and fulfill a purpose bigger than ourselves. Only such a larger purpose can inspire us to heights we could never reach on our own."

— *Os Guinness, author*

Steps on the Journey

1. When you hear talk about being part of a journey with God, what reservations come to your mind?
2. What excites you about what God might do through such a journey?
3. Consider two or three values you genuinely hold to and build your life upon. What are they?
4. What personal comforts are especially difficult for you to part with?

Speaking to God: *Lord, open my heart to understand the greatness of your plans for me. I want to know Christ and the power of His resurrection, the fellowship of sharing in his sufferings, and whatever else You have for me. Be my leader and companion for the journey ahead. Amen.*

Prayer Log—What is God saying to me?

chapter one

We Are People
of the **Gospel**

The memory of my first roller coaster ride as a boy still gives me chills. An unwitting fourteen-year-old, I was psyched at the thought of getting into that coaster car and having the ride of my life. My friends and I planned this adventure carefully, imagining all the spins and twirls, the speed, and the enormous opening drop with great detail.

When it was our turn to ride, I knew where I wanted to sit. "Real men" rode in the front car. The safety bar came down with a thud, and we crept up the opening hill. As we neared the top, random thoughts raced through my head. *What was I thinking? The hill is higher than it appeared. Is there any way out of my predicament? I wish I hadn't taken the first car.* But it was too late.

Years later, I find myself crossing international borders pondering the same thoughts.

One trip in particular proved a breathtaking experience. It began with a phone call from a friend who led a significant ministry in the Middle East. "Hey Steve. I was just thinking about you. I heard about a man with a vision to reach his nation with the gospel and plant churches. I don't know him yet. Would you be interested in checking it out and perhaps being a part of making

1

church planting a reality in his country?" I was about to board another roller coaster.

My friend spoke in sketchy details, but I was already aware of the nation as a hard place, not particularly friendly toward Americans, and high in spiritual need. Some people groups in that region had no known followers of Jesus, so with thoughts of a possible leader to pilot this initiative a team was soon on a plane.

In many ways, the entire experience was surreal. Maybe unreal is a better description. We were separated at the border and placed in rooms for a brief "conversation" with a soldier carrying a weapon that looked more formidable in real life than on TV. The soldier's words were abrupt and sharp, his face stern as he walked back and forth.

"Why are you here? Why do you hate us? Who are you going to see?"

I tried to look relaxed, although it didn't help to see the walls of the building riddled with bullet holes. Was this some defining moment when I should boldly proclaim the gospel to this soldier? Was this meeting a divinely appointed opportunity for spiritual advancement?

"I don't know," and "Can't remember," followed a few compliments toward the soldier to dispel suspicions. My responses grew less heroic as I stumbled through replies. My stomach tightened and dropped just like that day on the roller coaster.

God Can Meet with You Anywhere

We met our contact, enjoyed great days together, and fell in love with the people of this nation. Months later we returned with a team to pray and meet with other believers embedded in the culture. As these national leaders shared their stories, we learned about a lost people group within the country numbering in the millions. Lost meant there were no known followers of Jesus from this ethnic group in the country; no known churches existed among them.

National leaders took us to a massive castle in the area where this people group lived. Now just to clarify, this was no Snow White kind of castle. There was nothing flowery or cute about it. It dated back to the twelfth century, the era of the Crusades when Christians and Muslims fought over territories and religious supremacy.

God can meet with you anywhere.

The castle was huge and stark in appearance. Its granite stones provided little color and transported me back almost a millennium in time. Inside, musty smells and dim hallways dominated. I peered through narrow openings in the wall and imagined the terror soldiers felt as arrows flew and hot oil flowed in those ancient battles. The scene reminded me of the ongoing spiritual battles of this region.

But we weren't visiting with historical interest. Climbing to the top, tears welled up in our eyes as our national leaders pointed out what they observed. "There are 481 villages out there," they said from this strategic vantage point. "And no churches. People need the gospel, but the work has been slow and hard." We spent the day on the castle, praying for the villages and for God to unleash His work.

I knew about the 10/40 Window for years. Mission strategist Luis Bush discovered an unusually disproportionate number of people without Jesus living in the area defined by the tenth and fortieth north latitudes. As he challenged Christians to pray and visit this region, the term "10/40 Window" became a focus of the missional community. Not only was I situated in that window, my head was sticking out of it as we called out to God.

The day possessed a bizarre but electric feel as I sensed the heart of our friends who desperately longed for God to reach their people. We experienced a sensitivity to God as we prayed. I perceived God's love for lost people in a fresh way as the courage and vision of our new friends encouraged us. I sensed a larger purpose unfolding.

That day I wondered if God would answer our simple prayers that seemed so enormously beyond our reach. How could a people group, who for centuries held nothing but negative images of Jesus, actually embrace Him? This put my core belief in the wonder of God's ways to the test. Could God be up to something that would unleash the gospel here? Perhaps you've faced similar thoughts with the people and situations of your life.

How Well Do You See?

I live in Colorado and love exploring the majesty of our state's mountains. As a hiker, I've grown to appreciate a compass, especially when my journey takes me to a new area. Initial steps of a journey require discernment with something like a compass to properly lead us in ways God wants us to go. Head in the wrong direction, and it doesn't matter how fast you travel. Wrong direction equals wrong destination.

Before we dive into the subject of following God, we must begin by asking some directional questions. When answered with the compass of God's Word, these questions will guide our lives well on the journey.

1. Who is God, and what is He up to these days?
2. What is His gospel, and why is it called the gospel (literally, good news)?
3. Who are we, and do questions one and two have anything to do with that identity?

My experience tells me Christians don't answer these questions in the same way, if they address them at all. I was often frustrated and confused as to why these basic issues of the Christian life were seldom addressed in the church, but I'm now

We each have a lens or filter to understand life events.

beginning to understand why we struggle. Uncertainty of life purpose and direction confuses many of us. Clarity revolves around a word that will need some explanation. The word is *worldview*.

The word *worldview* sounds complicated and maybe a bit philosophical. In a sense it is complicated because of the complex nature of people and how we think. However at its center, *worldview* conveys a simple concept, namely how we see life. We each have a lens or filter to understand life events. That lens doesn't always provide an accurate picture; nevertheless, life experiences continually pass through the lens of *worldview*.

Question One: Who is God, and What is He Up to These Days?

I'll use an example to illustrate the importance of this first question. During one of our global trainings in Peru, this issue of *worldview* was front and center in the class I taught. The class, comprised of pastors, church planters and other leaders, was a quality group of God's people. Soon it became clear, however, the group struggled to grasp the character of God. Some saw Him as loving. He was a harsh, mostly angry God to others. In fact, the majority saw God as a judge in the extreme. Serve Him or else!

I decided to work through the story of the Prodigal Son in Luke 15. Instead of teaching through the passage, I suggested we act it out. Soon a ready and willing person volunteered to play the part of the Prodigal, while I would be the Father in Jesus' parable.

As we acted out the story in this impromptu sketch, tears flowed from the eyes of the Prodigal as I (the Father) welcomed him back into the family. I thought, *This guy is a terrific actor.* He captured the emotion of the son's return extremely well and everyone in the class was engaged. As I continued expressing the Father's heart toward His lost son who returned, my acting buddy broke down in sobs. The entire class, including me, kind of "lost it."

We took a break, and I spoke with my volunteer. "What just happened up in front of the class?"

His response was pointed. "I grew up in a family where Dad was rarely home, and when he was, my brothers and I were often beaten in his rage. I once even asked my Dad if he loved me, but he couldn't say he did. I guess I grew to think God was like my dad. So when you put your arms on my shoulders and told me you loved me and accepted me, it was the first time in my life I ever experienced anything like that. It hit me for the first time—I was loved after all."

I offered thanks to God for making that class more than an academic exercise. God used it to release a young man from the bondage of guilt in serving a hard-to-please God. This story also captures a person's worldview. His view of God was inaccurate and affected everything else in his life.

He saw God as a harsh, uncaring judge, and his vision of the Christian life became distorted. Legalistic duty defined life; grace and joy were absent. The only good news in the gospel for him was a slim hope: if he measured up before God, he wouldn't have to go to hell forever. As you can imagine, he also struggled with how he viewed himself. Life experiences and even the Bible passed through the lens of his worldview.

How we see life, God, the gospel, and ourselves give insight into how and why we operate as we do. Simple solutions as to why Christians or churches struggle in this missional arena or why they lack vision miss the point. Every one of us has values and a worldview that frames life and defines who we believe we are.

God understands this and provides a helpful biblical pattern: behavior flows out of our worldview and values.

The New Testament letter to the Ephesians is one clear example among many. The end of the letter (chapters 4-6) contributes some of the greatest teaching about honesty, dealing with anger, holy living, loving family relationships, and kindness. The teaching is pertinent and practical, but before the writer dives into all the necessary behavioral admonitions in his call to action, he spends three chapters (Ephesians 1-3) explaining worldview.

Majestic instruction on God's nature and His relationship to us fill these early chapters. The Apostle Paul says we need to put on a decent pair of glasses, a clear set of lenses before anything else. See who God is. See who you are. See the good news of how it all happens. God knows that must come first; then we can talk about how to live.

Question Two: What is the Gospel?

We struggle with our understanding of the gospel as well. At least this was my experience. I'm grateful I was taken to church as a child. However, looking back, I now understand my neighborhood church struggled with the gospel. We heard a lot of sermons about hell, which taught me hell was certainly a place I didn't want to go. I experienced guilt and shame as weekly services were often

7

inquisitions with some group or denomination taking a hit during the message. But I was loved by people there and I learned Jesus died for my sins and I could go to heaven if I accepted Jesus. That was the gospel to me.

What I learned was true but not complete. My worldview regarding the gospel was distorted. In fairness, this may not have been intentional. I learned the gospel was a message people needed to hear and believe. After that, you moved on to understand doctrinal fine points and Christian duty. Discipleship was step two in the process; getting people saved was the first and most important step.

Years later, I stood on the other side of the pulpit. What I observed disturbed me — much focus (sometimes heated) on doctrinal correctness and precision and, sadly, little energy directed on life transformation.

I wondered why the gospel wasn't changing people's marriages, for example. Researcher George Barna's work demonstrates no definable difference in permanence between marriages of self-identified born-again Christians and nonbelievers. Why weren't the relationships of professing Christians different? Why was the integrity of Christians underdeveloped? I wondered if the problem rested not on the gospel's power and ability to transform life, but upon how I viewed the gospel (my worldview).

Could it be the good news of the gospel extends beyond hope for the future in heaven, though that is truly good news? Could it be the gospel speaks to more than forgiveness from past sins at the point of salvation, though we desperately need that? To be sure, I understood the gospel implied repentance and faith, turning from sin and trusting Jesus as Savior.

However, there's even more good news to the gospel, namely we continue to live in repentance and faith. I learned there's an ongoing work of the gospel; the gospel is how we live.

This isn't a discussion about losing salvation. We need to understand the gospel and its power. This ongoing work of the gospel delivers us from our sins and continues to call us from lifeless, purposeless lifestyles that distract us from the journey. In a word, the gospel transforms.

What else could the Apostle Paul have meant when he declared if anyone is in Christ, he is a new creation; the old is gone, the new has come (2 Corinthians 5:17)? The gospel is about life transformation. As my friend missionary Mark Hendrickson puts it, "The gospel is not only about getting people into heaven; it's about getting heaven into people."

> *I learned there's an ongoing work of the gospel; the gospel is how we live.*

Jesus understood the nature of the gospel and continually emphasized its present power. When the woman caught in the act of adultery was brought to Jesus, He underscored the gospel in His words to her.

> "Neither do I condemn you ... Go now and leave your life of sin."   John 8:11

Steven Childers, the president of Global Church Advancement, focuses on understanding the transforming power of the gospel. He explains the nature of the gospel well. "The gospel is not just a gate we pass through one time but a path we are to walk each day of our lives. The gospel is God's solution not only to our guilt, but also our moral corruption."

Childers continues, "The gospel is not merely a set of propositions to be believed and defended, but it is also a supernatural power to be released in and through our lives and churches for a broken world."

In our church context, we often hear that we need Jesus today just as much as when we first came to faith. I believe that. We approach all of life in a posture of repentance and faith. We'll see the implications of comprehending the gospel in this way in the next chapter, but for now, it's important to note this ongoing transformational power of the gospel.

Question Three: Who Are We?

This third foundational question concerns our identity. How do we see ourselves? If we believe the compass of our identity points toward having little value, with little or no connection to what God might want to do, then our lives will generally detach from the journey God charted for us. Live life, get through it, and move on to heaven. But is that accurate?

As I write, I'm also reading sweeping portions of God's Word. What jumps out at me is how often God reinforces issues of *worldview*. He wants us to know who He is, the greatness of His plans, and also who we are and how we fit into those plans. Likely the frequency of these themes in Scripture reflects both our slowness to embrace our identity and the importance of this truth.

As I read through Peter's first letter in the New Testament, I'm touched with the challenges these early Christ followers faced and their frailty as people. Life was hard, and the people were not always up to the task, yet Peter's message addressed their identity and mission.

"But you are a chosen people, a royal priesthood, a holy nation, a people belonging to God, that you may declare the praises of Him who called you out of darkness into his wonderful light." (1 Peter 2:9) He later referred to them as aliens and strangers in the world (which sometimes made their identity feel less certain). This was not only true for our brothers and sisters of past centuries, but something God wants us to know about ourselves today.

God thinks you are somebody, and He believes you have a significant role in what He's doing. Have you ever considered this about yourself?

God reinforces our identity in the Bible. We're people given the privilege of telling others what God can do. Jesus called us "witnesses" who will take the gospel to people in ever-widening circles until the good news reaches the remotest people group (Acts 1:8). He commissioned us as multipliers of the gospel, investing in would-be disciples among all people groups (Matthew 28:18-20). In fact, God names us "Christ's ambassadors" to represent Him and His interests in the world (2 Corinthians 5:20).

God thinks you are somebody, and He believes you have a significant role in what He's doing.

We Are People of the Gospel

When considering the issue of identity, I like to say we are "people of the gospel," in that the gospel characterizes how we live. The word gospel literally means good news. This word is used in varying forms ("good news," "proclaim good news," or "one who proclaims good news") some 133 times in the New Testament. D.A. Carson, seminary professor of New Testament, is correct in noting, "because the gospel is news, good news, it is to be announced; that is what one does with news."

The early Christ followers who received the commission first-hand didn't miss Jesus' intent. These first 120 understood their identity and also understood the nature of the gospel. Their number quickly grew to

3,000, then 5,000, then many more. The gospel spread far beyond their home base in Jerusalem to Samaria, Africa, Turkey, the Mediterranean, and Europe.

God desired the gospel be unleashed in a dynamic movement across the world. This good news affected the religious, irreligious, hate-filled legalists, those in authority, and common people. It all happened through people very much like you and me: people who understood they were people of the gospel. They knew what God could do, because they understood who God was. They preached, healed, and cared; sometimes they died.

When compared to those who came before us, we may feel unworthy, maybe overwhelmed. We may feel very ordinary. I understand those feelings and identify; however, these feelings need not be where our stories end.

A few years ago I noticed a change in my eyesight. Words on a page were blurred and too small to read. I wondered if publishers moved to smaller font sizes, but the problem was mine. I needed glasses to read and from the moment I looked through the proper lens, life changed. I could read again.

In the same way, God offers us a different set of glasses. They're not magical, just basic equipment for the journey ahead. These glasses provide a clear and accurate view of God and help us see ourselves in fresh ways, closer to how God sees us. These glasses sharpen vision and, in the process, redefine "ordinary" and show us what is possible.

God Can Do the Extraordinary

A year passed before I returned to the Middle East and the location of our castle prayer gathering. I was eager to see our friends. Our national leader told me someone wanted to meet me. We packed into his car and drove through a series of back roads. I realized something was up as he kept asking in Arabic if anyone was following us. Certain we were alone, we finally arrived at an out-of-the-way restaurant where we met a man. As we ate, Ahmed (not his real name) began to speak.

Ahmed seemed common and soft spoken though he was a person of position among the people group we were praying for. That piqued my interest and so did his story.

"One afternoon a man suddenly appeared to me in a vision," Ahmed said. "The man in the vision said He was Jesus."

Ahmed's story caught my attention as he detailed Jesus' call to follow Him. Ahmed was very awake through the vision and spoke clearly about what he saw and heard.

"Others in the vision told me not to follow the man, but I fell at Jesus' feet," he said. In the vision, Ahmed expressed his desire, his faith as it were, to follow this Jesus.

"I told many people about my vision and taught God's Word to many," he continued. "Many family members came to faith in Christ; some sheiks even joined our number."

A church began, the first known fellowship among this people group. God answered our prayers and the prayers of many others. For Ahmed, a journey with Jesus began that would impact many.

I was moved as I listened to the story told very humbly, quietly thanking God for what He initiated. From this simple beginning, a movement grew, and courageous leaders developed. People of the area heard the gospel; they've also seen the gospel through practical acts of love and God's deliverance. Opposition and danger have been part of the journey but have

13

been overshadowed by new churches. The gospel is being unleashed.

I now realize the similarities between that early roller coaster ride and what I experienced on my journey. With moments of apprehension came satisfaction and joy in seeing God at every turn. That's something I'd never trade and something that awaits us all.

"We must see the difference between choosing to serve (an activity) and choosing to be a servant (a lifestyle). When we choose to serve, we are still in charge . . .when we choose to be a servant, we give up the right to be in charge . . .we become available." — *Richard Foster, author*

"Fear of the future causes present blindness."
— *Erwin McManus, pastor and author*

Steps on the Journey

1. Think about the three questions of this chapter and your personal response. Describe in just a few words your worldview as it relates to:
    a. Who God is (How do you see Him?)
    b. What the gospel is (How do you see it as good news?)
    c. Who you are (How do you see yourself?)
2. Look through your responses to question one, and evaluate them in light of God's Word.
3. How does being identified as a person of the gospel affect you?

Speaking to God: *Lord, clear away the misconceptions of my past when it comes to seeing you and seeing what you have for me. Teach me more of who you are and who I am. Fit me with a lens that sees what you see. Thank you for choosing me in Christ before the creation of the world to be holy and blameless in your sight. Amen.*

Prayer Log—What is God saying to me?

chapter two

Finding Purpose
and Hope

Some moments change everything. Decisions and actions can set into motion a subsequent series of events, often taking us in a whole new life direction. Marriage or childbirth affects us in this way. Christians likely include their experience of faith to follow Jesus. The significance of life moments is not always evident. Sometimes we know the implications of our actions; sometimes we do not.

For Abraham and Sarah, such a moment came when God told Abraham to leave his country, people, and family, and pursue a journey with Him to an undefined destination. Did Abraham understand the implications of his journey? Could he have comprehended the life impact for him and his wife? Or did he have any idea of what he would miss if he had declined the invitation? All we know is Abraham obeyed, with some sense of future anticipation and hope from the God who called him, but no real knowledge of what lay before him on the journey (Hebrews 11:8-10).

Those first twelve followers of Jesus faced the same issue. Knowing Jesus, they anticipated something positive in terms of outcomes, but specifics about what the journey might look like . . . well, they received only a curt "Follow Me" response from Jesus (Mark 1:16-20). That's not much of an information dump! Could they have understood or imagined what the three years ahead would look like? I doubt it. We don't even know if they grasped the import of following Jesus (personally or for others) or what their lives would have been like had they said no to the offer.

Those are the real life issues we all face on this journey. Presently we don't know what lies ahead, any more than Abraham, Matthew, John, Martha, or the others. We possess only a sense that God desires to unleash His people with His gospel in order to bring hope to the world He loves. God invites you to the journey.

This brings us to discern those life points that redirect and change our lives in significant ways. For our church, that occurred on Father's Day, 2005.

From the outside, circumstances leading up to that day were not especially unusual. Ministry was going well. In fact, there was a lot of good work going on both inside the church and in the community. Without major crises and armed with favorable attendance and offerings, the American benchmarks of a successful church, we were generally a happy church family.

Reservations surfaced however through voices that reached the ears of church leadership, voices almost prophetic in sound. One person saw the church like a big, expansive tree with many branches but no leaves. Another pictured the church as a room with many seats, all filled, but with mannequins rather than people. Neither vision was especially flattering. Their impression was we were losing our love for Jesus and just involved in activity. As spiritual leaders, our first impulse was to say, "Interesting, but that's not us. Look at all the good things we're doing."

Fortunately, we took time to seek God about this. Praying He would show us if this was accurate, many of us sensed these words were true. On that Father's Day, our lead pastor Alan Kraft essentially tore up his planned message and spoke from his heart about what we were processing as leaders. He called for repentance. It proved to be an eventful weekend, as people acknowledged fading love for Christ. Many came forward to the front to express repentance and desire to follow Christ. When the dust settled, other issues stood before us. Clearly we had grown comfortable, doing only what we could accomplish in our own strength.

Clearly we had grown comfortable, doing only what we could accomplish in our own strength.

We had become a church that was playing it safe.

That day defined us in many ways and led us into an adventure that dramatically changed us. As we prayed about what to do next, we realized we needed to understand our dependence on God. Ephesians 3:20 became a sort of biblical mantra.

Now to Him who is able to do immeasurably more than all we ask or imagine, according to his power that is at work within us.

We named our next church-wide effort Project Beyond and asked the congregation to give resources toward kingdom work that would extend far beyond what we could do ourselves. We gave above our usual tithes and offerings, but more significantly people gave of themselves toward ministry in extraordinary ways.

People stepped up in acts of commitment, often in line with their latent passions to serve Christ as they had been gifted. None of us knew where this journey would take us but we knew God was up to something. Project Beyond and what followed exploded far more than we could have imagined. We saw God's activity, Ephesians 3:20-style, in motion. It still continues years later.

Discovering Adventures in Real Life

Significance results when people see their purpose. Energy emerges when we know we're involved in God-orchestrated activity. When God's grander purpose aligns with how He made us, the effect grows in power. As people took steps in the journey, I could see a difference in them; I also saw a difference in me. I felt alive, as if I'd uncovered the reason I was created. The journey intrigued me.

The journey took us many places, both near and far, generating new relationships. Project Beyond provided an opportunity for our people to connect in areas of personal giftedness. That giftedness proved broad and diverse. Whether it focused on health care, construction, teaching, counseling, evangelism, or working with children, we saw God using our abilities for His purposes. God used our lives, with strengths and limitations, to make a kingdom difference. Many sensed *God can use me!*

One unexpected example of how this developed early on: amidst the variety of needs, marriage seemed to stand out. We came face-to-face with cultural practices globally which degraded women; this distressed us. As people embraced the gospel, we learned unhealthy family patterns were not easily overcome. (This is nowhere more true than in our own culture.) This lack of transformation troubled us even more as we listened to people's pain.

Our first venture in helping marriages came unexpectedly. We met with a group of Christian leaders in the Peruvian highlands. Following a nice lunch, my wife Karin and I were introduced to them. We really had no idea of the real intent of the meeting.

"So," the leader began. "We would like you to help us with our marriages. How can we assist our people if we aren't doing well with relationships ourselves? We came to this marriage conference to learn from you." The words "marriage conference" didn't need to pass through our translator. I looked at Karin like a deer in headlights. We both heard it. So we were suddenly leading a marriage conference?

While it wasn't the greatest presentation on record, God came through. These leaders were fascinated as we shared our hearts and how God had worked in our own marriage. Hope lit up their faces.

Later we led a team with skills to address marriage issues in Africa. This time we were prepared, or so we thought. Upon arriving we were informed the tribal leaders didn't want to come with their wives. Right away, we sensed it would be a strange marriage conference. Later, they relented on the condition they wouldn't be asked to sit next to their wives or sleep in the same rooms. This was going to be tough!

The conference started poorly, as you can imagine. Nothing connected, and finally we separated the men and women and just talked. What followed pained us—women expressed deep hurts and anger, how they shared their pastor-husbands with prostitutes, beatings they received, and terrible loneliness. As the men talked, passive-aggressive behavior surfaced, which they had elevated to an art form. The men thanked us for coming but plainly told us we didn't understand marriage very well. "Women aren't people," they said, "only property."

Some adjustments to the plan were obviously needed.

We gathered the group, set the notes aside, and shared our hearts and God's Word. God did a work, and by the time we ended we noticed husbands serving meals to their wives. Alarmingly, many of the wives nearly fainted from the shock of this new experience. One couple ate off the same plate and commented, "You spoke of our oneness in Christ; we want to demonstrate that by sharing the same plate together." Years later we met some of these couples and rejoiced in the progress we witnessed in their lives.

At a similar marriage conference in South America, couples began to dance together in response to the teaching they were applying, resembling couples at a prom they never had. It took our team an hour to make our way back to our cottages just a hundred yards away due to all the singing and dancing. These were beautiful moments, as gifts, passions, and God's favor came together.

Everyone wins when we see the reason for our lives, as the journey possesses life-giving and enduring qualities. This is precisely what Jesus had in mind in communicating God's purposes, sometimes choosing metaphors to define our journey.

Imagine Water Flowing from You

John's Gospel records Jesus at the Jewish Feast of Tabernacles inviting anyone who was thirsty to come and drink (John 7:37). The availability and sufficiency of Christ is in itself a profound truth. However, Jesus provides significant insight to help Christ followers understand themselves. His words ring with impact:

> Whoever believes in me, as the Scripture has said, streams of living water will flow from within him.   John 7:38

Most of us have no problem attributing this metaphor to Jesus' life and character. Certainly we would agree that streams of living water flow from Jesus. He is the giver of life, providing life abundantly and freely. But here's the challenge. Jesus was not speaking of Himself but us. Jesus takes this picture of life-giving water and depicts it even more graphically flowing out of us! Streams of living water flow from those who believe in Jesus, that is, people of the gospel.

At the beginning of this book, we talked about the Niagara Falls. The thunderous outpouring of water and its benefits to people portray the gospel. The gospel in its very nature brought an outpouring of God's blessing to people wherever they might be. Jesus chose the language by design. Living water *flows* from us, not to be restricted to a trickle or drip. It also flows from *within* us, as a natural and organic overflow of the gospel pouring out of our hearts. Nothing need be coerced or pressured. Jesus intended the gospel to be unleashed in this way.

Jesus' listeners struggled to comprehend his teaching on how God would use them to provide living water to others. I can identify with those who felt overwhelmed with such a high calling. Perhaps you join me in thinking *Who is adequate in themselves to provide living water to others?* Fortunately the Gospel of John added a valuable footnote for explanation.

> By this He meant the Spirit, whom those who believed in Him were later to receive. Up to that time the Spirit had not yet been given, since Jesus had not yet been glorified.   John 7:39

John connects Jesus' words of life-giving water to the Day of Pentecost in the second chapter of Acts when the Holy Spirit was given to believers. Note the connection.

Followers of Jesus need God's supernatural power in them in order for His life-giving water to flow from their lives. Fulfilling God's purposes isn't a matter of abilities or skills. The Holy Spirit

Fulfilling God's purposes isn't a matter of abilities or skills.

filling people of the gospel make Jesus' words a reality.

I began to see the relationship between this truth and my purpose. From the day the Spirit was given, and through the entire book of Acts, awesome missional expansion occurred. Water flowed out from these early people of the gospel because the Holy Spirit lived in them. This occurred spontaneously, and the church grew and the gospel advanced in powerful ways. Stories within the book of Acts provide a detailed narrative of what happened as these early Christians were filled with God's Spirit.

This much is clear: wherever these early believers moved, "streams of living water ... flow[ed] from within [them]." Salvation, forgiveness, healing, and hope resulted.

Imagine Light Shining from You

Light provides another metaphor to clarify our purpose. When Jesus' parents brought Him to the Temple just eight days after His birth, a godly man named Simeon spoke over the child. In language quite prophetic, he said Jesus would be a light for revelation to the Gentiles (Luke 2:32). This statement likely sounded extremely strange to all the devout Jewish hearers who may have wondered if that word, "Gentile," was complimentary or not.

Matthew quotes Isaiah, the prophet, in regard to Jesus saying, "the people living in darkness have seen a great light" (Matthew 4:16). John's take on Jesus' work is similar.

The light shines in the darkness, but the darkness has not understood it.   John 1:5

Jesus self-identifies with this metaphor.

I am the light of the world. Whoever follows me will never walk in darkness, but will have the light of life.   (John 8:12)

There's an obvious observation about light and darkness. When they're in the same place at the same time, light always wins. A light shining brightly in a room can't be overcome when it gets dark outside. In fact, light's value increases in darkness. However dark a place may be, light illuminates everything.

We love the metaphor of light when it applies to Jesus. Anyone who follows Christ finds His words true as He dispels our darkness. It's as if He lifts a veil covering us so we might walk in the light of His truth.

But again, here is our problem. Describing *Jesus* as the light of the world is not especially challenging. Accepting what Jesus says about *us* often is difficult— very difficult. In language wonderfully similar to what we just read in John 8, Jesus says,

"*You* are the light of the world."
                    Matthew 5:14 (italics added)

An incredible identification with Jesus takes place. He is the light of the world; we are the light of the world. He shines; we shine. It's an identification of purpose, a description of the gospel that brings light.

We need to talk about light a bit more, just as Jesus did, because it relates to our journey with Him. He explained,

A city on a hill cannot be hidden. Neither do people light a lamp and put it under a bowl. Instead they put it on its stand, and it gives light to everyone in the house. In the same way, let your light shine before men, that they may see your good deeds and praise your father in heaven.

Matthew 5:14-16

When you follow Jesus, you become a person of the gospel. You become light to people all around you, bringing benefit and blessing to everyone who needs it, just like light brings hope for those in darkness.

Connect your missional purpose to light. Jesus couldn't conceive of a person lighting a lamp in a dark room and then covering it. It equally makes no sense when we, the light of the world, conceal our works and silence our words that give praise to God. Light by its nature benefits everyone who comes in contact with it. Like water, this natural, organic purpose frees us from pressure of duty. Light and water refresh.

I deeply appreciate the many people who join us on our teams. They demonstrate high levels of commitment and love. Our philosophy is that light is especially needed wherever it is dark. So we have chosen to go to difficult places, where the light of the gospel is obscured or non-existent, and bring hope. Move toward those in darkness.

How Do Water and Light Work?

One time, our team served in a remote jungle area. Some worked in schools. Some connected with people and shared God's good news. Health professionals saw hundreds of people, providing practical help for those who needed their skills.

People in the region faced issues without easy cures, so teams of intercessors trained local native intercessors and prayed over anyone who desired God's help. These were ordinary people who prayed for whatever needs they observed.

Many found hope and healing, and the word spread throughout the nearby communities. It

It shouldn't surprise us if our journey takes us into new territory.

wasn't unusual for people to say, "My friend was healed here yesterday. He said Jesus did it. Can you tell me who this Jesus is?"

My purpose in sharing this is not to rattle any theological boxes (okay, maybe a little). Rather, life-giving water and light goes wherever God sends it, often to dry and dark places. It shouldn't surprise us if our journey takes us into new territory. God accomplishes what He desires in any way He chooses.

A friend works in a dangerous Middle Eastern city. Many have come to faith as he has prayed for their healing or deliverance. Clearly God does it, yet God has chosen to work through our friend in ways uniquely suited with His plans.

Light and water must flow from us as well.

So then, how do we proceed? I believe three approaches help us advance God's kingdom work as water and light. Perhaps they are best illustrated from the model of Jesus who explained His own purpose. Early in His ministry, Jesus read a passage of Scripture in the synagogue.

> The Spirit of the Lord is on me, because He has anointed me to preach good news to the poor. He has sent me to proclaim freedom for the prisoners and recovery of sight for the blind, to release the oppressed, to proclaim the year of the Lord's favor. Luke 4:18-19

Quoting Isaiah 61, He added a comment that made for one of the more interactive synagogue services at the time.

> Then he rolled up the scroll, gave it back to the attendant and sat down. The eyes of everyone in the synagogue were fastened on Him, and he began by saying to them, "Today this scripture is fulfilled in your hearing."   Luke 4:20-21

Kingdom Approach #1: Proclamation

The first way the kingdom of God advances is by using words to communicate the message of the gospel. God anointed Jesus to preach and proclaim. Not surprisingly, Gospel accounts reveal Jesus preaching the good news of the kingdom in towns, villages, and synagogues (Matthew 9:35). In religious, irreligious, and everyday settings, Jesus proclaimed good news. The message of Jesus' death on the cross for us and His resurrection can change a person's heart.

We have learned that genuine, caring relationships opened doors for us to share the gospel with little or no pressure. The old adage is true: "People don't care how much you know until they know how much you care."

With poetic eloquence, the Apostle Paul expounded on the relationship of love and proclamation:

> If I speak in the tongues of men and of angels, but have not love, I am only a resounding gong or a clanging cymbal.   1 Corinthians 13:1

We make a helpful delineation in our attitude as we proclaim God's good news. I'll illustrate. Years ago, some local churches protested our school district because they wanted the curriculum to reflect biblical values. When the district resisted the churches' agenda, Christians mailed angry letters and distributed hate-filled leaflets that only resulted in greater distrust.

In this fortress approach, lines are drawn between people needing the gospel and people possessing the gospel. Both sides highlight their differences and use skillful arguments against their opponent. Fortress thinking attacks what we dislike, often with hostile words and actions, to protect our interests and values.

But could we take another approach? Paul wrote,

> Through us [Christ] spreads everywhere the fragrance of the knowledge of Him.
>
> 2 Corinthians 2:14

He then describes Christ followers as "the fragrance of life" in 2 Corinthians 2:16 — a *fragrance* instead of a fortress.

We began to ask how we could be the "aroma of Christ" to our school district. In response, Christ followers volunteered to mentor children. We purchased sports equipment for under-privileged students. During a stressful time in the school district, we provided Starbucks gift cards to over a thousand school staff with notes of appreciation. These weren't gimmicks, but expressions of support for our teachers and students.

Kingdom Approach #2: Power

In His purpose statement, Jesus spoke about freeing captives, giving sight to the blind, and releasing the oppressed. He knew the kingdom advances through power. Not only did Jesus preach, He healed every sickness and disease, even freeing people from demonic oppression. Jesus saw a clash of kingdoms taking place, a battle of cultures involving a real enemy, Satan. We know our king won this battle, however, it materializes in real life today as part of everyone's journey. We enter into darkness as light, sometimes displacing darkness that has been undisturbed and entrenched for a long time.

Areas of darkness don't always welcome light—as we've experienced on several occasions. Some of our African partners work on the Uganda-Congo border. Arriving in the area, we sensed the darkness of spiritual oppression, as it remains geographically isolated from gospel advances, even today. The few who follow Christ often face spiritual attack. People steal babies and sacrifice them to appease their gods and bring favor. Senseless tribal conflicts routinely kill dozens and disperse fear. How do people of the gospel respond?

A combined team of over one hundred Ugandans and Americans walked area roads to pray. What a day, filled with setbacks, frustrations, and strange events that weren't in the plan. But God worked as people found healing in Christ. One leader of sorcery in the area professed faith in Jesus. In repentance, he burned the articles of his craft as songs of praise were sung. Light entered into the darkness.

Kingdom Approach #3: Sacrificial Love

As Jesus shared His mission, He surrounded His miracles and message with sacrificial love. Supremely displayed at the cross, this sacrificial love was the context for all that Jesus did.

> When [Jesus] saw the crowds, He had compassion on them, because they were harassed and helpless like sheep without a shepherd.
>
> Matthew 9:36

Sometimes when I'm trying to develop a strategy for a mission project, I think to myself, *Okay, what would Jesus do if He were here?* We can answer that question in various ways, but compassion always forms part of the solution. Love sets us apart as we embody the fragrance of Christ by loving others in a way that permeates a community.

Sacrificial love motivates church teams in our Colorado community as well. Men and women fix up the homes of widows. We provide oil changes for the cars of single moms, free of charge. We teach English classes for refugees and immigrants. Couples adopt children who need homes. We provide relief to local families who've experienced the ravages of a flood. Sacrificial love holds such a high value to us that we also release an army of people into our community to bless them with projects in homes or local schools.

Love sets us apart as we embody the fragrance of Christ.

We want to develop this culture in our church — a culture of light, a culture of water. I recently read a magazine article which researched Compassion International's program of child sponsorships. They sought to determine if sponsoring children in places of high need made any difference in everyday life issues like education or employment.

The results were astounding. Child sponsorships make a huge and lasting difference. The researcher visited with Wess Stafford, then president of Compassion, for follow-up. "I think there is something deeper going on in the program that would interest the greater development community. I need some leads." Stafford simply replied, "Try hope."

When you live out the gospel, like water in a dry place or light in darkness, you bring hope! Such a journey begins with a moment.

"I felt as if I were walking with destiny, and that all my past life had been but preparation for this hour and this trial."
> — *Winston Churchill, statesman on being asked to lead his nation against the Nazi onslaught*

"I'm a little pencil in the hand of a writing God who is sending a love letter to the world."
> — *Mother Teresa, servant of Christ*

Steps on the Journey

1. Identify two or three defining moments that changed your life. What would your life look like if you had taken a different path?
2. Assess your life today. Are you aware of people or situations calling for God's hope? What are those situations that especially tug at your heart? Who are those people?
3. Identify yourself as water or light in those situations. How might you proceed?

Speaking to God: *Lord, I desire to let my light shine before men, that others may see my good deeds and praise you in heaven. Allow me to see the significance of my daily life. Help me identify those people and situations that I may act on your behalf. Amen.*

Prayer Log—What is God saying to me?

chapter three

The Making
of a **Visionary**

One of my best friends in the world possesses extraordinary vision to see what others cannot. He grew up in a religious cult and blamed capitalism — especially the American version he saw on television — for the injustice and poverty he witnessed in his South American country. As a result, he turned to terrorism. He viewed our country as people of wealth who exploited the poor for their advancement, and as a result grew cynical and angry.

Through a vision, God uncovered his pain and revealed what Christ could make him. Following his conversion, Juvenal led a group of multiplying house churches where many came to faith. However, he always thought in larger spheres and pictures. If the spiritual gift of vision exists, Juvenal has it.

I met Juvenal shortly after he came to faith in Christ. The two of us remain quite a pair. Neither of us cared much about maintaining programs. Juvenal nearly fell asleep during any administrative discussions at meetings, but if someone even whispered reaching lost people or strategic ways of extending the kingdom, he rose from the dead. We saw each other several times a year as teams assisted the work of establishing new churches, and near the end of each time together, Juvenal and I walked and talked through dusty neighborhoods. Juvenal's insights inspired me.

On one visit, we travelled to a faraway outpost community called Cruz del Norte, which essentially existed as an open space of dirt and sand. No services like water, electricity, or health care existed at the time to assist the thousands of people who lived there.

"What do you see?" I asked Juvenal as we stood on a small hill overlooking the area. Obvious answers to that question included "not much" or "a group of Satan worshippers on the next hill over." People who fled terrorism arrived in Cruz del Norte for a measure of safety that came with a mass of people surrounding them. I knew what most would have seen that day: *"Oh my, where are we and what are we doing here?"*

"There's no church here," Juvenal responded differently. We both saw little joy in this place, and no one to help.

I thought out loud, "Something tells me our team will be coming here soon."

Juvenal just smiled. Then we prayed over the area that God would pour out His Spirit upon this dry and thirsty place.

In a few months God answered that prayer, and our church was privileged to be a portion of the answer. We invited people to join us to provide medical and dental care plus talk to people about the One who had hope for all who were thirsty. Many responded and Cruz del Norte came to life with spiritual energy.

One afternoon, a weary group of us walked back to the clinic area for something to eat. Trekking through one particular area, our eyes were drawn to a simple home of woven cornstalks tied at the corners with wire and covered with a blue plastic tarp. We were all exhausted, but someone suggested we stop at this last house. We knocked on the door, and a young woman answered.

As I looked at her, I sensed years of pain in her weathered face. She lived alone with few possessions well placed on the dirt floor of her home. Her eyes seemed to speak of hope, or maybe bewilderment of her strange guests.

We introduced ourselves and the reason we were there as we got acquainted.

"Last night I had a dream," she interrupted us. "And in the dream, I was told Jesus would come to my house today!"

After a few speechless moments, the team shared that we had come in Jesus' name. Obviously, she was eager to hear the good news. Not only did she commit her life to Christ, but joined us in sharing with others about her own personal relationship with Jesus, which began earlier in the day. The community turned out for a dramatic baptism service later in the week — Christian and not-yet Christian alike witnessing the stories of people who had come to faith.

When we left, a newborn church was infected with Juvenal's vision. Within twelve days, this new church sent a mission team to Ecuador. They planted a daughter church in a neighboring community, then another, until three generations of churches existed in the area within a year. It was yet another picture of a church unleashed. It all began with one man's vision.

Jesus Possessed Remarkable Vision

Jesus constantly astounded others with what He saw. Intimately connected to the Father, Jesus' eyes picked up on people no one else noticed. He saw inside their hearts; others were oblivious to such things. He saw opportunities when others saw impossibilities. Matthew 9 highlights this. When I first studied this chapter, I noticed the repeated use of the word "saw" especially in contrast to the observations of others around Jesus. My vision sharpened as I discovered Jesus' perception of people around Him.

This ninth chapter of Matthew represented a busy time for Jesus. While we don't know exactly how much time is covered in these events, the narrative reads as if one event follows right after the other, the transitions in the passage giving the impression there was a flurry of people and activity filling Jesus' day.

Jesus first "saw" something no one else noticed in the second verse. With the help of Mark's account of the same event (Mark 2:1-12), we know people in that Galilean community observed a group of men cutting a hole in some guy's roof. Then they lowered their disabled friend through the hole in order to get a front row seat before Jesus in the packed house. Most people noticed this disturbance. They likely resented the roof's dried mud falling on their heads. But Jesus detected faith. He forgave sins and healed the disability.

Jesus constantly astounded others with what He saw. Intimately connected to the Father, Jesus' eyes picked up on people no one else noticed.

Next Jesus "saw" a man named Matthew (Matthew 9:9). Everyone recognized Matthew as a prominent tax collector of the region. But they hated him because he contracted with the Romans to collect tax revenue for them along with a healthy bonus for himself. While people saw a traitor, Jesus discerned something else inside Matthew. Perhaps it was faith or just emptiness, or maybe Matthew longed to be part of something significant God was doing through Jesus. Jesus saw it and invited this tax collector to be His follower.

Later Jesus received the sad news that the daughter of a ruler had just died. The news came with a bold request. Would Jesus come and touch the girl's dead body so she might live again? Jesus consented.

On the way to the ruler's home, a woman who suffered from a chronic bleeding condition worked her way through the crowd to touch Jesus' robe, believing her action would heal her. Most that day would hardly notice the woman, as she was one of many sick people with health issues beyond the scope of what medicine could provide. She might have been viewed as an annoyance or distraction to the ruler's dead daughter. But Jesus "turned and saw her" (Matthew 9:22). He saw her! With a note of personal encouragement and acknowledgment of her faith, Jesus immediately healed her.

The eyes of Jesus continued to see that day. As the entourage entered the ruler's home, Jesus, "saw the flute players and noisy crowd" (Matthew 9:23). People hired musically gifted people to mourn at funeral events, so again no one would have regarded anything out of the ordinary that day, except Jesus. Perhaps they were just poor musicians, but more likely Jesus saw the inappropriateness of their presence in what was going to be a very happy time. Jesus dismissed the band, took the girl's hand, and raised her to life.

Still another incident emerges in this chapter. While the word "saw" is not used to describe what took place, ironically it involved Jesus healing two men. Their physical blindness pictured in principle the disciples' inability to clearly see what God observes. Perhaps you struggle with vision as well.

The ninth chapter of Matthew concludes with a summary and personal footnote about vision.

When He saw the crowds, He had compassion
on them, because they were harassed and helpless, like sheep without a shepherd.

Matthew 9:36

The disciples saw just crowds, lots of people who
rocked the level of their comfort with their endless needs.

If you're like me, you can probably identify with
these early Christ followers. At times they asked Jesus
to send the crowds away. People can wear us down,
unless we see differently. As Jesus looked at the crowds,
He saw helpless, leaderless people and compassion
welled up within Him.

Vision Can Be Corrected

Jesus saw people in unique ways, raising the
question "why?" Why was Jesus able to see them so
differently from most of us? Vision is a function of
worldview. Vision is connected to how we, at our core,
see life. Let me ask you a practical question to illustrate
this: How do you see your community? What is going
on in your city as you see it? How might your vision
compare to Jesus' vision?

A political organization in our city asked me to
speak to them about my experiences in the Middle East.
Fears were starting to run pretty high that an Islamic
takeover of our community was underway. I wondered
about the strategic nature of this happening in our city,
but nevertheless the fears were present. At a previous
meeting of this group, someone asserted that Muslims
had already taken over schools, and now churches and
political structures were under attack.

Actually I was quite aware of radical Islamic
elements in the world, more than the crowd realized.
However, I saw things another way and challenged the

group to see Muslims differently. "Could it be possible," I asked the audience, "that God brought Muslims to our community so we might love them and reach out to them?" The group struggled with my suggestion. Their worldview needed to be addressed.

How do you see your community? Our city of 105,000 people is home to large Latino and refugee populations. People have come from over 40 nations of the world, speaking some 19 different languages. Your community may be different though many American and western cities have experienced similar demographic changes. Some in our community resist this influx. In some ways I understand this as political, social, and educational realities make life more challenging.

Perhaps the better question to ask: "How does Jesus see my city? How would He respond?"

But are those social perspectives the best way to see your community? Perhaps the better question to ask: "How does Jesus see my city? How would He respond?"

Vision concerns our worldview. It concerns how we see through the lens of God's heart, which provides a valuable filter in discerning life and can lead us to see opportunity. I often tell people interested in missions, "You don't have to go any farther than across the street. God has brought the world to us. Do you see it?" Deep friendships have developed with people from both our refugee and immigrant populations, as we have grown to see each other differently, hopefully more as Jesus does. God is at work.

A Case Study in Vision

Did I lose you in this discussion about vision and Jesus? After all, Jesus is Jesus. As God, He is capable in this area of vision like no one else. But take heart, for I hold to my premise that ordinary people possess vision for the journey, and we have many models of those who have gone before us to help. I particularly like Nehemiah of Old Testament fame.

Nehemiah interests me for many reasons, one being that he wasn't the spiritual leader of the people. His colleague, Ezra, who held the role as priest and teacher of God's Word, stands as more pastoral in rebuilding Jerusalem following hard years of exile. Nehemiah's specialty was construction management, with training in quality control of the king's food and drink in case someone wanted to poison him. In many ways Nehemiah was an ordinary man spiritually, yet the development of his vision skills became legendary.

Nehemiah experienced a life moment that changed everything. As a Jew working in the Persian government, he found interest in an earlier group of exiles that had gone back to Israel. One day, he received a firsthand report from a small group of returning exiles. The report described Jerusalem's situation as a disaster.

Early resettlement went poorly plus the city walls (which symbolized a city's strength) were demolished, leaving people vulnerable to enemy attack. The situation in Jerusalem screamed loud and clear that the people were nobodies. Morale crumbled.

That news report triggered something in Nehemiah. As we follow his story in the biblical book that bears his name, we see the development of vision in this man. We also see help for ourselves in this same area. Notice how it begins:

When I heard these things, I sat down and wept.
For some days I mourned and fasted and prayed
before the God of heaven.   Nehemiah 1:4

Nehemiah's initial response is important for any of us seeking to be unleashed in the plans of God in this world. Time with God proves to be indispensable. For sure, the bad news broke Nehemiah's heart. Those were his people, his relatives, and his friends who suffered. He wore his emotions on his sleeve at this point, for when Nehemiah returned to work, the king's first words to this servant were, "You look terrible," or something to that effect (Nehemiah 2:2).

In his grief, Nehemiah went to God. For days, he didn't sleep much nor eat at all. Curiously in his heart's cry before God, he didn't gripe or complain or rant about the lack of leadership in Israel. He identified with his people and confessed his sins—his own as well as the people's.

Nehemiah's life illuminates an essential point. It's difficult to see the world as Jesus does without consulting Jesus first, humbly seeking His heart and identifying with those in need. However, journeys include both coming to Jesus and going, taking steps of action. For Nehemiah it meant approaching his boss to request time off so he could venture on a mission trip to Israel. Without this bold step of action, Nehemiah's vision would be nothing more than a wistful, passing thought.

So the vision came alive for Nehemiah as he travelled to Jerusalem and saw the situation first hand. Now he gazed on rubble where great walls once stood, observing the ashes of once-strong gates. This firsthand look made the vision clearer, reinforced as Nehemiah secretly rode through the wreckage at night, likely processing with God what he saw and considering what could be done.

If you desire to have vision and see others as Jesus did, there's no substitute for experience. Volunteer to help serve people in need. Ask questions; get to know them. Travel to that place of need in the world or in your city. Talk to the people, and listen to their stories. Hearing the reports of others is important, but first-hand exposure elevates vision. It might break your heart or move you to tears, or even drive you before the Lord in fasting and prayer as it did Nehemiah. Discomfort may result; yet your vision develops when you see people in real life — in their pain and need. Those moments can be life-changing.

After Nehemiah travelled the city wall and experienced the hardship, he returned to the people with his vision. He honestly acknowledged the city was in sad shape, as well as the bigness of the task and the risk. But Nehemiah shared something far more valuable — vision. Vision inspired the people, reminding them with God's help the wall could be rebuilt; their future could be different.

If you know the story, you'll recall the construction project wasn't easy. But fifty-two days later, the people had rebuilt the wall, returned to God, and hope was restored. This extraordinary feat transpired through the vision of an ordinary man.

You Can Change Your Worldview

Understanding worldview and its link to vision can be more of a challenge. I tend to notice faults more readily in others. Removing a speck in another's eye is easy; dealing with this log in my own is something I want to avoid. But there is another, even more basic and troubling question we must address: Is it even possible to change my worldview? Can I see life more as Jesus did or is that only in the category of "when I get to heaven"?

We grow accustomed to seeing life and people a certain way. If we wear glasses with dark blue lenses long enough, we convince ourselves that the whole world is dark blue — and no amount of persuasion by others will change it. Fortunately our Great Physician specializes in ophthalmology.

The early disciples provide a helpful case study in this issue of vision. Throughout the Gospel accounts, they suffered from severe vision impairment. When people refused to give them the respect they felt they deserved, they called down fire from heaven. They complained about people doing good deeds when not under their supervision. They pushed children away from Jesus and experienced a meltdown during a stormy night at sea. They preferred arguing about personal greatness over washing feet in an act of service. They just didn't seem to see it. Their glasses appeared to have the letters "ME" written on the lenses.

I find their example hopeful though personally convicting. Strangely, their defining moment occurred after Jesus left, when He filled them with the Holy Spirit in Acts 2. At this point, significant transformation occurred in their lives, including seeing life differently. On the way to a prayer meeting in the Temple, a disabled man asked them for money. Peter and John's response was powerful.

> Peter *looked* straight at him ... Silver and gold I do not have, but what I have I give you. In the name of Jesus Christ of Nazareth, walk.
>
> Acts 3:4-6 (italics added)

You Can Receive New Vision

To me, the insightful part of the story was not only the powerful healing but also how Peter and John saw the man. They viewed the disabled man as their Lord Jesus would have seen him. Their experience at Pentecost changed their worldview, and in turn, their vision. That's the other miracle of the passage.

That worldview became a new way of living and seeing throughout the book of Acts (with a few setbacks along the way). We find Peter hanging out with hated Samaritans (Acts 8) and even associating with Gentiles who become his brothers and sisters in Christ. We can't really comprehend what a huge shift in worldview those events represent!

What made the difference? Two practical truths stand out. Most importantly, the Holy Spirit makes the difference. What we could never do ourselves, God does in us through the promised power of the Holy Spirit. Called our teacher and guide into truth, the Spirit's work produces fruit like love, joy, and peace, which affects our vision and relationships. Through the Spirit, we are born again, this time with better sight.

Through the Spirit, we are born again, this time with better sight.

Training also makes a difference. Changing your vision is not a matter of trying harder. The Christian life is not a series of attempts to try to be better Christians or to squint more fervently to see people as Jesus did. It does not follow the old adage "If at first you don't succeed, try, try again." Instead the journey places us under Jesus' leadership. As we read His Word and acknowledge our weakness and need before God, He trains us toward Christ-likeness. He exposes us to new habits and new vision. Transformation results.

I love seeing vision develop. One of the early initiatives under our church's Project Beyond work was the establishment of a ministry centered on coffee. I confess my love of coffee played into this, but the vision of others made it happen.

Phil, one of our staff leaders, desired to connect with a part of our community that was either indifferent to

Jesus or previously burned by unhealthy church experiences. He eyed an old, tattered nightclub in town that was once a beautiful brick building.

To be honest, you'd need vision to pursue the facility as the nightclub hosted some ugly and violent activity, including a murder just before we took ownership. But our leaders saw something. A coffee house came together under good leadership that connected us to the community in beautiful ways.

These leaders saw something even bigger. They loved to roast their own coffee. So why not get coffee beans from our international partners, some of whom we discovered had coffee ties in South America and Africa? We call it "direct partnership coffee." Only people with vision could have seen the connection.

We now work alongside coffee growers, and relationships develop where growers receive a fair price for their product, which allows them to support themselves and ministries in their own country. This includes church planting in needy areas and involvement in social problems such as trafficking or family issues. The results: communities are blessed, the kingdom advances, and I get a really good cup of coffee.

It all flows out of vision. Can you see life and people more as Jesus does? How does your worldview change to make that happen? The next chapters tell us how.

"All men dream; but not equally. Those who dream by night in the dusty recesses of their minds wake in the day to find it was vanity; but the dreamers of the day are dangerous men, for they may act their dreams with open eyes to make it possible."

— *T. E. Lawrence (Lawrence of Arabia),*
soldier and author

Steps on the Journey

1. Vision is important as God creates His desired impact through our lives. What scares you about vision?
2. Read Matthew 9 again. How might you see the people that Jesus encountered that day? Are there any personal tendencies you notice in yourself regarding initial observations of people?
3. Vision has been referred to as an outside perspective on the present. Identify areas that you tend to see differently from Jesus. Ask God's Spirit to adjust your spiritual eyesight in these areas.

Speaking to God: *Spirit of God, I need you. Be my vision. You see past the externals to know the hearts of people. Please shape my own heart. Forgive my narrowness of vision that often focuses too much upon myself and too little upon your ways. Give me a picture of what you desire for me to see and do.*

Prayer Log—What is God saying to me?

chapter four

To Follow Christ Means to Follow Christ

Some images remain indelibly etched on my mind. Sabina waded through chest-deep water deep in the heart of the Amazon rain forest. With a small pack held above her head, this middle-aged Peruvian woman braved a piranha-infested river because she heard of a tribal people in need of the gospel. My personal disdain for piranha or being eaten by an anaconda or whatever lurked in those muddy waters left me out of the picture I've described. But not Sabina!

She and the team arrived in the tribal community on the eve of an execution. Three men committed a crime deemed worthy of death by tribal leaders. The Peruvian team requested permission to speak with the condemned prisoners. Hearing the gospel, the trio responded with faith to this savior Jesus.

Meanwhile, the observing tribal community wanted this good news as well. A work of God's Spirit resulted in new life and the birth of a church. The community faced a dilemma, however. "How do we now kill these prisoners who've now become our brothers in Jesus?" Newfound forgiveness flowed through repentance, and pardon was extended.

Commitment to Christ Touches All of Life

Working with church leaders around the world can be an awesome and humbling experience. In Africa, we worked with a team of church planters who minister in some of the most spiritually hostile environments toward followers of Christ. As we arrived, we learned a leader in this team was recently murdered for his faith. Another worker's daughter was crucified (literally) due to her identification with Christ. The conversation among these church planters was somber, yet strangely matter of fact. I learned what the Christian life looked like in their context.

My emotions were exposed as I processed what I heard and saw. I loved these new friends and was inspired by their passion for Jesus. Inwardly however, I struggled as we prepared to send workers into an area of the world with similar levels of danger. I agonized about this, sensing the weight of perhaps sending people to great harm if events went poorly.

I talked with the leader of this church-planting organization at length. As an American Christian leader, I believe the Bible's words about being crucified with Christ or the importance of laying down my life in serving Jesus. I even believe Paul's words:

To live is Christ and to die is gain.

Philippians 1:21

But I had reduced all these great statements into metaphors, into concepts and ideas that preached well. In reality, most Christ followers in America don't live under the threat of death because they identify with Christ. The most helpful words came from my friend Aila who leads this indigenous African church planting work. "Steve," he said, "you must remember that to follow Christ means to follow Christ."

What about the "R" Word?

We must talk about the challenging subject of risk. On a practical level, we as a church typically enter areas of ministry with caution and discernment. However, to be honest we really don't know where this journey with Christ might take us or what might happen.

Christian living generally, and the missional edge of following Christ specifically, is the story of God's Spirit working in and through us. He leads; we follow. While we don't always talk about it, that work of God isn't solitary. Others matter. We connect with and invest in the people woven in and out of our lives. And God's interests stand front and center.

For example, a spiritual war rages as God advances His kingdom against the kingdom of darkness and its evils. During His earthly ministry, Jesus consistently clashed against the work of the evil one who enslaved people and caused pain. That battle continues and with it risk, which always accompanies such serious struggles.

Hebrews 11 fascinates me as God presents a case for trusting Him through numerous examples of people exhibiting faith on the journey. The phrase "by faith" rings out in a litany of honor to those who chose the journey. By faith, Abel did this and Enoch did that. Noah, Abraham, Moses, and company did what they did by faith. Great adventures, like crossing the Red Sea or leveling the city walls of Jericho, were accomplished by faith. Military victories, miracles, and resurrections followed faith. Who wouldn't want to sign up for such a life?

However, almost seamlessly, words we don't like as well follow in Hebrews 11. Words like torture, imprisonment, and death are presented frankly in more graphic detail than we would prefer. The last verses of the chapter are hard to read. Sometimes living by faith is painful. We know Jesus wins and we with Him, but before the end, many experiences can happen—not all of them good. Deep down we know this may keep us from following Christ.

Risk from Jesus' Perspective Brings Freedom

In some ways, this is another of those worldview issues we've talked about. When seeing risk through Jesus' eyes, freedom results. Risk is simply part of the landscape of life. Of course, there'll be opposition to face, resistance to encounter, and problems to overcome. Why would we think these would not be the case in our situations? History gives us a record of risks, the Bible underscores this reality, plus everyday life confirms this as true. The latter part of Hebrews 11 did not really catch God off guard, nor did people's rejection of His Son or the crucifixion. Jesus calls us to view risk differently or better, to see risk as He does.

Ordinary people who view risk through the lens of the gospel bring forth extraordinary impact.

Ordinary people who view risk through the lens of the gospel bring forth extraordinary impact.

To see risk properly, we must understand the present set of lenses we're wearing. Most of us in the West view risk as an anomaly, but this wasn't always the case. It certainly isn't the way most of the world thinks. We tend to see risk as foreign. We think risk and danger shouldn't exist, especially with a God who loves us. Following Jesus ought to be easier and happier.

I once asked a Middle East leader about the dangers facing our brothers and sisters in his part of the world.

"All Christians face these kinds of risks where persecution is present, don't they?" he replied.

"Frankly," I said, "we're unaware of persecution in our part of the world. We desperately need your insights."

Comfort Can Be Our Adversary

American churches tend to shy away from risk and cling to what is comfortable. We buy comfort and have developed a variety of gadgets to meet our comfort demand.

Recently our aging vehicle died, so we purchased a new car. It was equipped with a special comfort— heated seats. We may see heated seats in heaven. They're incredible on a cold winter morning. And yes, I really did say, "I don't know how I'd ever live without them again." Comfort is alluring.

The problem lies in transferring this value to the church or the Christian life. The attraction to comfort can be deadly, creating a brand of Christianity that is passive and disengaged from the world God calls us to. Jesus repeatedly sent His followers into tough places, with early churches advancing in strange and sometimes hostile cultures.

Sadly, today too many have retreated into safe places to do safe ministry in comfort-controlled environments. We have become somewhat monastic, cloistering like medieval Christianity in the face of being swallowed up by pagan cultures, "safe and secure from all alarms." Even some of our hymns betray us.

Comfort's danger lies in a posture of retreat—not risking involvement, which can create inconvenience or discomfort. At a time when global issues cry out for Christ followers to engage and when the gospel is desperately needed in our own nation, we tend to become invisible. Perhaps others will do it, so we wait for others to lead. Again, this is understandable if we acknowledge the worldview from which we operate. Our addiction to comfort remains strong.

Of course, the irony is that the truly risk-free environment doesn't exist, whether we're Christ followers or not. Even Adam and Eve, who lived comfortably in an environment as good as it gets, faced deadly risks in the form of one particular tree and one difficult snake.

The attraction to comfort can be deadly, creating a brand of Christianity that is passive and disengaged from the world God calls us to.

But good news emerges as we honestly address this issue of risk. The reality? Risk isn't the same as fear. While every life journey includes some element of risk, fear is a response we can either embrace or reject. Fear is clearly a powerful emotion that easily impacts us; however we need not be enslaved to fear. We need not *live* in fear.

The most common biblical command, repeated over 300 times in various forms, is "Don't be afraid." That is, fear is a response, a reaction to situations of risks. When faced with fear, God calls us to assess the situation in light of His presence. Biblical David captured this in his experience in the twenty-third Psalm:

> Even though I walk through the valley of the shadow of death, I will fear no evil, for you are with me; your rod and staff, they comfort me.

While people of the gospel can become afraid or struggle with issues of fear, it need not dominate or control how we live. There's another way; there's hope.

You Can Move Past Your Fears

Andy and Courtney are a young couple who, following graduation, anticipated moving to the Midwest to pursue graduate studies. They're a gifted couple with a heart for God and a love for people. After they married and started to pursue the plan, God indicated His journey would take them in another direction. They listened and obeyed. Instead of leaving, they stayed.

They moved into an apartment in a complex where many refugee families lived, especially Burmese people who had endured persecution in Myanmar and then camps in Thailand. Andy and Courtney joined the refugee community. By their own admission, they faced a sharp learning curve crossing cultural and language chasms yet enjoyed their new neighbors. They opened a resource center to connect with families and tutor the children. They arranged trips to the zoo along with other new experiences for refugee families. Most importantly, Andy and Courtney loved the people.

After some time, our church began an international campus bringing together various ethnic groups for worship. Plenty of challenges existed with diverse people coming together, speaking several languages with varied music styles. Those challenges continue today, yet something beautiful occurred in that diversity as well. Then one Sunday, ten of their Burmese friends expressed faith in Andy and Courtney's Savior. Was this whole endeavor risky? Sure, but they wouldn't trade the experience.

Next consider Colette, a wife and mother of three. Several years ago, a sudden influx of refugees came to our city, from dozens of countries, several religious backgrounds, and numerous languages. As you might imagine, they didn't integrate well. They faced significant issues adjusting to our healthcare system, work schedules structured unlike anything they had experienced, and education in an unknown language with subjects that seemed irrelevant. The refugee community found itself with few resources and even fewer advocates.

Meanwhile Colette had taken a course at our church aimed at identifying spiritual gifting and interests. Her results screamed "missional," so she volunteered to help refugees transition in their new community.

A leader emerged from within the refugee community, but with so many needs, small facilities, and no help, it was like climbing a mountain for him. Colette wanted to help, so she devoted many hours each week to develop the work. She recruited volunteers to teach English, offer general diploma classes, and even instruct citizenship requirements. Not many spoke English in those early days.

Within two years, her hard work resulted in the formation of a non-profit organization called the Global Refugee Center, of which she is the co-executive director. The center serves hundreds of people each week in education, case management, and practical assistance. It has become a model recognized at high levels of government to help transition refugees to contributing members of our community.

Loved by so many, Colette's participation made a difference. She was even recognized as an "Everyday Hero" on a major Denver television news station. Colette is an ordinary woman with a love for Jesus and a willingness to take a risk. Her perspective on all of this was amazingly simple. "It's all so much like God. This is my calling. God has placed me here. It is almost as clear as receiving military field orders." Serving is Colette's journey and joy.

Recognize Your Level of Risk

Risks wear many faces. One is in the area of giving. Some places in Africa where we work face severe famine. Driving through Maasailand and into the Rift Valley of Kenya hit our team especially hard one summer because it had not rained in a long time. As the spring rains failed, crops also failed. Cows resembled nothing more than skin loosely draped over bones, lying on the side of the road groaning and eventually dying.

Risks wear many faces.

One of our partner churches was especially hurting as six of their children had recently died from lack of food. I saw a woman peeling bark off lifeless trees to put something into her stomach. This image has not left me, as these were people we knew and cared about. While not a relief organization, our people back in Colorado responded generously and soon we brought truckloads of food to them, enough to keep families alive for a month or two longer.

As we approached the famine-stricken Maasai church, an eerie atmosphere encompassed it—dusty, barren, and totally quiet. I wondered how these people would respond to their loss and pain. Would they be bitter? Angry? Lifeless like those photos we've all seen in magazines? Driving closer we began to hear music—the beautiful strains of African lyrics. The church was packed with a couple of hundred worshippers praising God, clothed in colorful Maasai garb.

Our friend Pastor Amos awaited us. After we spoke and worship continued, our team distributed food. Looking into people's faces after all they'd suffered and hearing their simple words of thanks moved us. After returning home, one team member held bake sales to raise funds for additional relief, and we also explored ways to approach this disaster in more sustainable ways.

Our people's level of giving raised a question. Would our generous relief offerings now result in lower offerings for our local church? Would there be "compassion fatigue," as some call it, where people just grow weary in their charitable giving?

These are really worldview questions. One worldview states there are only so many resources available. It is the belief of a closed universe where money once given means those resources are gone and less will be available. But what about a different belief — that God provides for our needs even as we give what we have? All this seemed risky at the time, but as a footnote I'd like you to know God intervened. Instead of decreased church offerings, generosity emerged.

Another risky area involves prayer. How do we pray? I am blessed with both an army of people who pray for me and a smaller core of friends who pray more specifically. I genuinely appreciate all who pray as I am dependent on how God answers.

I'm amused at one particular prayer people express when I return, "I'm so glad to see you. I prayed every day God would bring you home safely." I know their hearts and am truly glad to return safely. But that's not the prayer I want offered. If the aim was to get home safely, then it would be easier to just stay home in the first place. I desire that God would do a great work for His glory, that He might even change whole cultures with the gospel.

Have you ever thought about approaching prayer differently? Someone once defined prayer as "rebellion against the status quo." I like that. We don't accept evil as normal, or assume the lostness of people is okay, or think sickness or despair is too bad but just the way it will always be. There's no presumption here. God is God and does what He pleases. I'm good with that, yet it's important to pray prayers of faith to God asking that He might change what is.

Many Christians are concerned about human trafficking. It's an evil like few others. As a church we've asked God to end this practice of selling children within the sex trade, and we pray more children would be rescued. We pray for God to change the hearts of people who need Him but don't yet realize it. That prayer was risky because God answered, bringing us into this battle along with others. Now it's part of our journey.

There's Freedom in Recognizing Fear

Risk exists in life whoever you are. We face fear as a result. But consider what your journey would look like if you made yourself available to do whatever Jesus has in mind. Period.

It might mean taking a mission trip to a far-off place or perhaps a mission trip across the street to your neighbors. What if we recognize how God's purposes have brought people groups to us? What if we take the risk of building an authentic relationship with someone unlike us? I believe opportunities hide behind risks.

Our response to risk matters. Freedom resides on the other side of risk, where fear loses its power and the kingdom advances. In part, I've come to see what's on that other side.

Here is a promise:

> For we do not have a high priest who is unable to sympathize with our weaknesses, but we have one who has been tempted in every way, just as we are—yet was without sin. Let us then approach the throne of grace with confidence, so that we may receive mercy and find grace to help us in our time of need.   Hebrews 4:15-16

While a bit of mystery surrounds the promise in terms of how it played out with Jesus, one thing is clear. God is present in our risk and fears, and Jesus experienced similar fears when He was tempted. He understands our dilemma, so we can come to Him with fears, failures, or whatever keeps us from being part of the journey. Coming to Jesus, we find both mercy and grace. That's the gospel! We trust Christ and get on with the journey.

Our response to risk matters. Freedom resides on the other side of risk where fear loses its power and the Kingdom advances.

A few years ago, our work in the Middle East faced a difficult moment. Persecution against believers in Christ and a national civil war generally made life risky. Our Middle East leader called together his leaders for a serious meeting, speaking what everyone in the room already knew. Reality pointed to some of them facing death or physical harm as danger increased in presenting the gospel to people. So he thanked them for their work and granted them a break until things calmed down. He loved them, and he understood if anyone wanted out.

These leaders faced risks. Most struggled with fears of what harm might come to their families, and so honest discussion was needed. Who would continue with the work? Before long, all of the group responded, "Yes, we are in. We'll continue, but we have two questions for you. One, where will we be buried?" (Issues of Muslims becoming Christians made them unwelcome in cemeteries. Since that time, they have constructed their own.) "Secondly, will you preach the gospel at our funerals?"

To follow Christ means to follow Christ.

⚬⚬⚬

"The response of a disciple is an act of obedience, not a confession of faith."
— Dietrich Bonhoeffer,
pastor martyred for his faith in Nazi Germany

"Every day you and I are making decisions that help construct one kind of world or another."
— Charles Colson,
government official and author

"Courage is more exhilarating than fear."
— Eleanor Roosevelt, former First Lady
of the United States

⚬⚬⚬

Steps on the Journey

1. We're only followers of Christ when we in fact follow Christ. Do you agree or disagree with this statement?
2. How would you personally assess your actual following of Christ?
3. On a scale of 1 to 10, with 10 representing total willingness to risk in following Christ and 1 representing complete safety guarantees, what number would you give yourself?
4. How has this issue of risk kept you from following Christ? How does Jesus' example in Hebrews 4:15-16 help?
5. What examples from the chapter helped you to see risk differently?

Speaking to God: *Jesus, in biblical days, you called people to follow you. Today I desire to respond with the commitment to follow. I am willing to do what you want me to do. Strengthen me in areas of personal obedience and generosity. Thank you for being both my Savior and Lord.*

Prayer Log—What is God saying to me?

chapter five

Surprises Come
in **Unlikely Places**

I'd like you to join me at one of the greatest places on Earth. While not very scenic, painted mostly in drab gray and brown tones if painted at all, and though remotely located in desert-like surroundings, I love it. Rules and restrictions number like mosquitoes in the Amazon; there's much you can't do and places you're not allowed to see. Masses of people, all men, mostly young, crowd into small cells they call home. I'm referring to a federal prison near Huaral, Peru.

There's a story behind the greatness of this place, involving hundreds of inmates and Christians on the outside. I entered the story about fifteen years ago because the husband of one of our church planters lived there. His name was Caesar. Though we had not met, many of our team along with our Peruvian friends prayed for him. He spent eleven years in Huaral for two reasons. He had committed a terrible crime. And through his brokenness, he found Christ.

Caesar emerged as a leader in the church-planting movement occurring in Peru after he was finally released from prison. One day he asked me to return with him to the prison where God changed his life. I asked, "For how long?" (I did want to clarify this important detail.) He assured me it would be for a brief visit only. So, joined by a handful of both American and Peruvian men, we ventured on our early morning journey.

First we received a few simple instructions—no belts, no shoelaces, just bring our passports which would be left with the guards. As we waited in long lines and tedious checkpoints with other visitors, we prayed that God would use us that day. We had no idea what to expect.

Security was tight. For two hours, we were searched, led through corridors of high chain linked fences and razor wire, and checked through a seemingly endless series of gates. We felt vulnerable, devalued, and exhausted through the process. In a scene of irony in this austere setting, prison guards stamped our arms with an assortment of numbers and press-on tattoos. The little bunny rabbit stamp on my arm didn't make me look especially tough, so our team certainly wouldn't be intimidating the inmates.

Finally we reached the room that would become our home for the next four hours, and the surprises began. At the front of Pod C, our destination, stood a beautiful mural of Christ the Good Shepherd. The words of Jesus in that shepherd role were painted in the picture. The sight lifted our spirits as our escorts ushered us through another gate and down long hallways lined with small eight-by-twelve-foot cells housing twelve prisoners in each.

Crowds of men followed us everywhere. Parenthetically we asked our host where the guards were, as none were visible. "Oh," he said, "It's not safe for guards to be in here." His explanation didn't reassure us.

I think God smiled.

Loud music—the recognizable sounds of vibrant Spanish worship—pulsated through both the room and us. Close to a hundred men were packed in a room designed for fifty to praise Jesus.

Literally no space existed to turn around or even move.

It was a church . . . in Pod C. As we learned later, many of those present became followers of Christ recently, some just weeks or a few months prior to our coming. Our host, Caesar, was highly respected.

Caesar was short, but muscular. His body bore scars of previous fights; his voice boomed with authority. Once the enforcer and leader in this place, following his conversion of faith in Christ, Caesar became their pastor and shepherd.

I tracked with Caesar the best I could with my limited Spanish. He spoke of real freedom that had nothing to do with bars and gates, but was found in Christ. Over the next hours, we sang, spoke, and shared our stories. The room grew unbearably hot and stuffy. Though sweat poured from all of us, nothing deterred the attention of the prisoners as we spoke. Joy filled their faces, and praise flowed from their lips.

Our team personally laid hands on each prisoner, praying over them. A refreshing breeze somehow accompanied our prayers. And to our surprise, these men wept like young boys held by the father they never knew. God's Spirit was at work and evident. Yet this was not the biggest surprise we'd discover in this place.

Faith Will Surprise You

Surprises have become normative wherever we work. I know God's surprises aren't the result of the gifts and abilities of our church family, though I deeply appreciate our people. In many ways we're ordinary. *Why us?* I've asked God on more than one occasion. *Why have we been so blessed to see the incredible activity of Your Spirit?*

I offer you no simple formula. Instead I wish to share something still mysterious to me, specifically the connection between faith in God and the surprises He brings.

The Bible presents faith in curious ways. On occasion, Jesus seemed amazed by the lack of faith in some people, particularly His own followers. At other times, He seemed overjoyed when unlikely people from different cultures trusted Him. People who expressed faith and those who didn't seldom fit any pattern.

Jesus often dropped out-of-the-box statements linking faith and the capacity to move a mountain (Matthew 21:21). Then He used the same illustration of rearranging mountain topology through faith but reminded His followers that faith cannot be measured in quantity. Faith resembling the smallest of seeds moves a person into the realm of seeing the impossible take place (Matthew 17:20-21).

Faith involves simple trust. And this trust is lifelong; we are always living in a position of dependence and trust in Jesus. Always!

Humility surrounds faith, for the wonder of faith seems to lie not in our effort to generate more of it or try harder to express it in greater measure. Nor is faith a matter of promising God that we will do better next time after we have faltered in believing Him. Faith involves simple trust. And this trust is lifelong; we are always living in a position of dependence and trust in Jesus. Always!

Saving faith, where we place our trust in Jesus as our Lord and Savior is vital, as it marks the beginning of our new life. Yet that faith, accompanied by a heart of repentance, is the uniform we wear throughout our journey. In the great faith chapter of Hebrews 11, we see people of the gospel commended for their ongoing trust in God, often expressed in very challenging settings when they faced hard decisions. Their initial steps of faith pleased God, as did their continued living out of that trust. God is delighted with people living by faith.

But what about you? Does God see you as a person who trusts Him as a way of life? Do you wonder if that's even possible? Or is a life of faith reserved for biblical heroes or religious professionals alone? The reality is faith is within reach of every person.

Though I enjoy sports, I fully understand I'll never be an Olympic athlete. I've worked through that. Ability or positions of prestige or having the world's most beautiful body or wealth in the extreme may be unattainable to many, but faith is something we all can be known for. It's possible that faith can mark the life of the rich and the poor, the old and the young, the fastest runner and the person confined to a wheelchair, the person from Denver or Delhi.

Faith Involves Forgetting

Years ago, a team prepared for a spiritually and physically stretching trip to Africa. As intercessors prayed over us, a staff member shared a passage of Scripture that proved powerful. It came from the prophet Isaiah as God spoke to His people:

> Forget the former things; do not dwell in the past. See, I am doing a new thing! Now it springs up; do you not perceive it?   Isaiah 43:18-19

I was startled by God instructing His people to forget previous things. Those "former things" of the past specifically mentioned in this section of Scripture pertained to God's miraculous work in bringing Israel out of Egypt under Moses. How do you forget the Red Sea experience? Their deliverance was a high point in

Israel's history, unforgettable if I can play on the wording of the passage. I doubted that the point was to erase all past memories and history. Rather with faith, we let go of the past in order to step into the future. It's almost like saying, "You ain't seen nothin' yet!" then building on what God has already done.

In the New Testament summary of Abraham's life in Hebrews 11, three experiences illustrate his faith. We already looked at the first one in Chapter Two—when Abraham obeyed God's call to leave the familiar and comfortable to pursue God's journey for him (verses 8-10).

The second experience centered around Abraham's belief that he and his 90-year-old wife would conceive and bear a son (verse 11). Giving birth to a son in old age was even more astounding because the couple remained childless after many years of marriage. Abraham's faith rested solidly on a promise God made to him. That promise was all he had to go on.

The third experience of faith focused on a strange command from God. Sometime after God's promise of a son, Abraham and Sarah gave birth to a baby boy. Now God told Abraham to offer his one and only son whom he loved and kill him as a sacrifice (verses 17-19). Likely, few of us could comprehend what Abraham did, much less reside in the same league as Abraham when it came to faith. The Bible says Abraham figured God would somehow, some way resurrect his son Isaac when the sacrifice was complete.

Note the progression in the passage. I think I could handle moving to a new place if God told me to relocate. Furthermore, having a child as I approached one hundred years of age is something my wife and I would need to discuss, but believing God in that scenario is possible.

But sacrificing my child … that's something else. Genesis 22 (the call to sacrifice Isaac) makes Genesis 12 (the call to leave home) look like faith-preschool. Yet Abraham never protested. We don't hear him venting about how he had already trusted God to leave his country and again to have a child. It certainly would be reasonable for us to think enough was enough. If it happened today, our prayer might be, *God, please give Abraham a break. He's proven His trust in you.* However faith meant more than passing the big exam and then moving on to the next course. It's ongoing.

Faith Involves Anticipation

Faith carries this constant forward-looking vantage point. Abraham was "looking forward to the city with foundations, whose architect and builder is God" (Hebrews 11:10). This again drives us back to our world-view and what we truly believe. Do we really believe God comes through in the end when our circumstances scream otherwise? Author Alan Hirsch put it this way: "Faith is the exciting venture in which we bet that God really is — that this is His world, and He is like Jesus Christ and He saves those who love Him with their lives." As a result, Hirsch continues, faith is more an act of courage than it is an act of knowledge.

Faith begins at a point in time. However faith progresses with continuing acts of trust in our heavenly father in all that comes our way. God calls us to see His new activity springing up in us, for faith continues new and fresh. We trust God each day, each step of the way like a hiker on a journey leaning forward in anticipation of what is ahead and less like a person sitting back in his recliner recalling what was in the past.

Jesus repeatedly called His early disciples to look forward. "Follow me," Jesus said (Mark 1:17). "Go and make disciples" (Matthew 28:19). "Go! I am sending you out like lambs among wolves" (Luke 10:3). "You will be

My witnesses" (Acts 1:8). Christ followers are called to nothing less than a journey where they keep trusting the One who called them.

Faith Involves Action

Another helpful observation about faith concerns the order of how it develops. I call it the sequence of faith. Typical of faith, perhaps by its definition, we first trust God before we understand how life turns out. Faith doesn't wait until all the ducks are lined up in a row and every contingency is addressed before it acts.

Faith doesn't wait until all the ducks are lined up in a row and every contingency is addressed before it acts.

That would be like Abraham, before agreeing to sacrifice Isaac, insisting, "First there needs to be a heart surgeon, a heart-lung machine, and eight units of blood on that mountain before I'll proceed."

The story of Gideon serves as another example of faith. God selected Gideon to deliver Israel from oppressive invaders from Midian. Gideon struggled to trust God in the assignment despite promises of victory. He wanted to be sure of those divine promises since God's plan of attack resembled a suicide mission more than a victory plan (see Judges 7). Gideon sought affirmation of God's victory through an experiment involving a fleece he laid on the ground.

The fleece part of the story doesn't seem to be a model for faith. I mean, God already told him what to do. A wet fleece in the morning lying on dry ground affirmed Gideon as did the following morning's dry-fleece-on-wet-ground scenario. God was patient with Gideon. It's curious that following the episode of the fleece, God reduces the number of Gideon's troops a couple of times, keeping Gideon again in a position of faith. Gideon rose to the task with the inspiring words to his remaining army, "Watch me ... Follow my lead" (Judges 7:17). God surprised them all with victory.

In faith, God pulls off amazing activity, but notice the sequence—God's surprises tend to follow faith. The present-day story of Bashar illustrates this sequence. Bashar (again not his real name) was an antagonist to our workers in the Middle East. Bashar was a powerful sheik in his sect of Islam as well as a lawyer. He used his knowledge of the Quran to attack the Christian faith, even threatening to kill one of our leaders in that area.

For five years, believers reached out to him with the love and message of the gospel. His response continued to be hostile despite their prayers and contacts. Even as their attempts to reach out to Bashar were growing more dangerous, Christians had faith he would come to know Jesus.

Then something strange began to happen within Bashar. Whenever he read the Quran, he felt uncomfortable and, in fact, extremely tired. This continued until, one night, Bashar grew especially unsettled in his heart. He went for a walk, reciting portions of the Quran for comfort but this exercise only made him feel worse. Returning home, he found a Bible Christians had given him and read it all through the night. He put aside the Quran and prayed, *God, I'm so sorry.*

Bashar knew Jesus wanted to save him, and his journey of faith was ignited on that July evening a year ago. He continued to read his Bible, memorizing the first eleven chapters of Matthew, and today a church meets in his home. He writes songs about Jesus who rescued him when he was dead and made him alive. Surprise!

I love Bashar's story, for it reminds me of God's ways—God's surprises follow faith. In fact, those surprises continue today. Jesus spoke a parable about faith in describing varying amounts of money given to servants by a master. One servant received five talents, another received two, and another a single talent. Each servant was endowed with a different capacity, but all were given similar opportunities. Each of them faced risk and, as you may know the story, each servant worked with what was entrusted to him. More accurately, two of the three invested the money, respectively doubling their master's investment. The third servant did nothing with the money and was fired from his job.

But before the master pronounces his judgment, Jesus gives us an interesting insight into His parable. The master says, "Take the talent from him and give it to the one who has ten talents" (Matthew 25:28). Then the point: "For everyone who has will be given more, and he will have an abundance. Whoever does not have, even what he has will be taken from him" (Matthew 25:29).

Elsewhere in the Bible, the principle is defined: demonstrating faith in relatively small responsibilities leads to being entrusted with more. For example, Jesus spoke of this in the context of money. "Whoever can be trusted with very little can also be trusted with much (Luke 16:10). Later, Jesus implied this involved more than financial considerations as He connected faithfulness in small matters to a future increased leadership role (Luke 19:17).

A life of faith-oriented decisions and actions opens the door to an extraordinary implication—as we grow in our trust in God, God knows He can trust us. As a result, God enlarges the scope of our work. And with our faithfulness comes surprises.

Every time I go to Peru, I look forward to returning to the church in Pod C at Huaral Prison, the greatest place on Earth. In fact, shortly before I began writing this book, I visited Pod C once again. When we arrived, we found nearly 300 men on their knees and on their faces before God for the first twenty minutes of the service. Then the praises started to ring out, nearly deafening in their enthusiasm. The Word was preached, testimonies shared, and joy was evident on the faces of the worshippers as well as interest from onlookers.

A life of faith-oriented decisions and actions opens the door to an extraordinary implication—as we grow in our trust in God, God knows He can trust us.

Believers now exist in the other seven pods (no, I don't know how the word got out). They gave an offering to support a Peruvian family who graduated from our International Training Institute and are now missionaries in western China. Their offerings also support prisoners with transportation and housing needs after they are released. Their goal is to reach each of the 7,000 inmates in the various pods of the prison— and asked if we'd like to come and help. As a result of the impact of these Christ followers, prisons throughout the country are encouraging this kind of ministry because violence in pod C has decreased, homosexual rape has decreased, and social behavior has improved. And surprise ... guards still aren't needed in the pod.

—⚭—

Pod C Huaral Prison is a picture of the transformative power of the gospel, the story of vision and faith, and the surprises God delights to provide.

"Faith, when we think about it, is not merely intellectual assent to a set of propositions, but the supreme gamble in which we stake our lives upon a conviction: It is closer to courage than it is to mere belief."   — *Elton Trueblood, author*

—⚭—

Steps on the Journey

1. Look again at the model of Abraham's faith summarized in Hebrews 11:8-19. What stands out to you in God's commendation of Abraham?
2. Note the progression of faith in Abraham, and that faith is not just a onetime expression when we come to know Jesus. What opportunities for faith have presented themselves on your personal journey with God? What might be that next step?
3. What is the relationship between risk, courage, and faith? Can faith exist without courage?
4. What most keeps you from expressing faith in God on the journey?

Speaking to God: *Thank you for giving me faith that unleashes surprises from you, Lord. Put me in a state of readiness to believe you and obey what you call me to do. In this, I need courage. I desire to continually grow in a genuine faith that results in praise, glory, and honor when Jesus Christ is revealed.*

Prayer Log—What is God saying to me?

chapter six

In Over
Our **Heads**

People have spoken three words to themselves to derail the best of journeys. Like a formidable detour barrier with flashing yellow lights, the words scream, "Stop! Go no further." Great plans and ideas have been set aside. Spiritual journeys ended. God-sized dreams forgotten.

What are these words? You've heard them, and they've likely crossed through your mind a time or two: *But what if … ?*

At some point, we've all sensed God putting something before us—an involvement that matters or an opportunity to serve Him. It may be a challenge to further His cause that stands before you. Perhaps He calls you to do something extraordinary, something out of your comfort zone, something new. You're excited, but then those words appear as if out of nowhere, sometimes blindsiding us: *But what if … ?*

What if something unforeseen happens? What if plans don't play out as expected? What if I fail on the journey?

I recall the confession of one team member following a positive mission trip experience. "On the morning we were leaving, I prayed I'd get sick so I wouldn't have to go. I got scared and wanted to back out. So many fears raced through my mind. I was hoping God would give me a good excuse to bail out on the team."

What If?

But what if ... ? goes beyond raising good questions or expressing honest concerns about what lies ahead. The statement focuses on making the journey contingent on figuring out every possible scenario and every minute detail. The statement originates in fear, looking for some reasonable justification to take us away from the journey God has for us. Often that dreaded fear of failing, of not being able to measure up to the task, surfaces in our minds.

More deeply, the question reveals insecurities in us, cracks in our worldview. It seeks from God a lifetime warranty for the journey, with total safety, happiness, and success written into the contract. But there are no earthly guarantees for this trip.

It's a bit like the old western movies as the wagon train headed west into a grand adventure only to opt for circling the wagons early on the journey instead.

Every journey—every life—contains an element of the unknown. Whether a person is a Christian or not, that's true. The natural trajectory of *But what if ... ?* thinking concerns me, for it leads to a posture of inaction. In any opportunity, this posture whispers to us: *I don't think you can do it. You don't know what might happen. Maybe sometime in the future, but not now.* I speak to this concern with a lot of compassion, because I've been there, but I'm also sad when I think of the impact that never happens or kingdom victories that are never won.

One of my favorite "what if" stories involved some wonderful friends who joined us on a mission opportunity. This particular trip promised serious challenges, but little did I know the extent of these challenges. We entered an area where terrorism reigned for many years against Christians. Churches had been burned, pastors killed and tortured. We knew much of the history of this region as we arrived; yet we were unaware cells of terrorism continued in some nearby communities. Our team arrived with positive attitudes along with tremendous unity and friendship. For many, the trip represented their first venture outside the United States with many new experiences presented to them. One particular morning stood out.

The unusual diversity of ministry made the day so memorable. My wife and another team member were asked to go to a place I never could pronounce, but is affectionately referred to by locals as "the place where Satan lives." A few believers resided, but no churches existed there, and the place had a feel of danger that kept gospel advances muted. The request came, "Would we go to share God's good news there?"

Other team members shared the gospel through the city. A few presented their stories on television. Everyone cared for people in practical ways. As part of the team headed into the city, their day took an unexpected turn. The team leader, JoAnne, another woman named Lina, plus their translator, Samuel, were impressed by God to visit those inside a prison in the city. (You may wonder if I have some strange obsession with prisons.) Typically, we wouldn't encourage two women to enter a prison, however sometimes God's leading becomes incredibly clear. That morning was one such day.

"We knew we were in over our heads." JoAnne later said. She, Lina, and Samuel arrived at the prison where they waited patiently for hours for entrance without success. The guards said no, but the women told them

God had given a yes. They insisted on entering. God always wins in those impasses, and finally they were allowed in, to their surprise, to a men's prison! The procedure was similar to other correctional facilities — checkpoints, searches, locked gates, and finally into the prison courtyard with again the absence of any guards.

Is this for real? JoAnne asked herself. *I thought this was a women's prison.* Then fear swept over her. The only man on the team, Samuel, was young and just as frightened as JoAnne. Passing by crowds of men in the prison, they entered a small cell with three prisoners. One man talked frankly about his evil past in excessive detail. Fortunately he also spoke of how Jesus changed his life and how glad he was to be in prison so he could tell others the good news of the gospel.

That evening we rejoiced as we listened to the stories of what God accomplished. And I thought, But what if ... ? What if we had said no and missed out on the activity of God that day?

The team of three then crawled through a hole in one of the chain link fences to another area, not knowing exactly where they were going or what was next. As they entered the area, JoAnne heard a group of inmates call to her: "We'd like you to preach God's Word!"

Into this impromptu evangelistic crusade, God placed JoAnne. She felt paralyzed, unable to talk. *Where is Billy Graham when I need him?* she thought. Yet JoAnne's voice returned and she delivered her "sermon" about Jesus. The gospel did its work that day, introducing half a dozen men to freedom in Christ.

That evening we rejoiced as we listened to the stories of what God accomplished. And I thought, *But what if ... ?* What if we had said no and missed out on the activity of God that day? What if promptings to visit that prison were ignored? It turned out that "the place where Satan lives" was now inhabited by dozens of new believers who trusted in Christ that day. Energized prisoners met in five new Bible studies that were birthed. Throughout the city new churches sprang up. But what if fears reigned?

You Can Move Beyond Your Fears

St. Francis of Assisi's conversion has always impacted me in overcoming fear. This nobleman, son of a wealthy merchant, described his life as rather detached and aimless, until one day while horseback riding through the countryside, he met a man with leprosy. His disease was well-advanced with horrific sores covering his body.

Normally, Francis would have ridden around the man, but that day was different. Something, or someone, drew him to dismount and approach the man. To his own amazement, Francis did the unthinkable: he gave the leper money to care for his needs, and then kissed his diseased hand! Biographers note that on that day Francis won the greatest victory a person could ever win—victory over himself.

Francis's story and impact went on to be extraordinary as we now know. He visited the local leprosarium, providing financial assistance and personal touch, which led to a movement of compassion globally. While we read these stories with amazement, they are actually the kinds of things God continually accomplishes as Christ followers work past their fears and the *But what if … ?* objections of life. They discover a surprising God able to do far more than they previously imagined.

Theologian Ted Peters provided a keen insight on approaching the *But what ifs … ?* of life.

Fear is a moral issue in so far as it shapes the kind of people we become, and the kind of people we become has a lot to do with how we see the world around us.

This insight brings us back to this whole idea of worldview. How do we see the world around us? Is it hopelessly evil? Dangerous? Rightfully on its way to hell? Not worth the risk to get involved?

Or do we see the world with a different set of eyes?

- As a Christ-follower, can God's power and purposes alter the wrongs I see?
- Does Jesus care about this world and its people?
- Am I a person of the gospel who lives as light and water in this dark and thirsty world, needed for precisely such a time?

This perspective determines our progress in overcoming fears and winning the victory over ourselves. Trying harder to be either less afraid or more courageous doesn't go far enough to provide the answers we need.

Ted Peters correctly explains, "How we view the world shapes how we act in the world." What makes that unique for Christ followers is that God is included in our view of the world; He's part of the picture. As Christians, His Spirit lives in us, and we live in continual repentance and trust, whether we succeed or fail. We're people of the gospel, with a God who is matchless in power, or as the apostle Paul summarized it, "God has not given us a spirit of fear" (2 Timothy 1:7 NLT). He has not given the spirit of *But what if … ?*

Understanding the Paradox of Fear

Centering God in our worldview puts fear in a different light. Albert Hirschman's writings intrigue me when it comes to understanding fear. A developmental economist, Hirschman loved paradoxes and was especially curious how various projects managed to succeed, both in spite of and because of difficulties.

An example he used was the building of the railroad in early American history across Massachusetts to the Hudson Valley and the West. Since the prosperity of the state rested on this project, quick approval was granted since everyone believed it would be a manageable project.

However midway into the huge venture, projections turned out to be faulty. The rock of the mountains was harder than anticipated, thus making it more costly to complete the railroad. Most every aspect of the construction process went poorly, and project costs soared. But something important caught Hirschman's analytical eye.

Engineers, literally trapped mid-mountain, understood it was now too late to turn back. They were forced to be creative and somehow finish the job, a project they likely would never have begun if they knew how challenging it would be. Upon reflection, the economist coined the famous phrase, "The shortest line between two points is often a dead end." That is, he saw virtue in the fact that nothing went as planned.

For sure Hirschman was innovative in the field of economics as his ideas flew in the face of prevailing thinking: challenges, uncertainty, and economic anxiety needed to be removed or diminished before projects are undertaken. Instead he felt there was no better teacher than adversity in producing successful habits and progress.

Whatever your views on economics, the principle for us as followers of Christ is clear—journeying with

Christ, even when an element of risk exists, drives us to trust God and to be creative in our actions. In fact, our own involvement in God's kingdom work often succeeds due to the difficulties we face as God proves to be faithful.

On several occasions, I've felt vulnerable during my own journey. As Project Beyond launched, I became aware of the possibility it could fail because everything was so new. As leaders, we navigated a steep learning curve with many of the projects to oversee. One national partner in Kenya wasn't honest with us in the early stages of serving the large functionally orphaned population of Africa. That disappointed me, especially in light of a friendship we enjoyed together for fifteen years. We had to end the project before it began.

There were also young and inexperienced Peruvian workers in Tibet moving around to literally stay alive as persecution swept through the area. They were in over their heads, but then we all were in various ways. I remember thinking this whole project could fail, and the church and I would look really bad. I needed to look at these issues of fear and failure differently, more creatively, and more biblically.

Seeing Fear Through Younger Eyes

My instruction in failure came from an unexpected source—children. Five years ago, I had my first grandchild and entered the era of grandparenting. Yes, it's grand, expanding my love for my family and my grandkids. The Bible calls your children's children a blessing; it's true. One of my observations includes my grandchildren's spontaneity and adventurousness in doing new things. Some of them are at that stage when they enjoy getting up in front of the family to perform. They exhibit an abandonment to just dance and sing, regardless of the setting or if the words to the songs are correct or if the dance moves are perfect. Those details never enter their minds. I love the delight on their faces and the humble "just do it" pleasure they exhibit.

Sadly, as we grow older, we also grow more self-conscious. You probably won't find me singing and dancing across many stages. While that's good for several obvious reasons, it reveals a sense of pride that we as adults have developed. We're constantly thinking, *How am I doing? What do I look like? What do others think about me?* The result is that we often retreat from situations and play it safe. We don't want to look foolish or fail, so we calculate carefully what we choose to be a part of.

> **We're constantly thinking, How am I doing? What do I look like? What do others think about me? *The result is that we often retreat from situations and play it safe.***

The danger surfaces as we choose a pattern of life to observe rather than do. After all, observing is safer than involvement. The simple unrestrained participation of a child is lost to a guarded disengagement from life. If this non-involvement was limited to merely singing and dancing, it would not be a big deal; but unfortunately it spills over into living our lives as followers of Jesus.

I needed to work through my own fears of not succeeding and constant concern of what others thought. It helped as I saw the response of early believers in the book of Acts in a new way. Like my grandchildren, they sang and danced the gospel before the world.

As Peter rose to speak on the day of Pentecost, he seemed indifferent to what the crowd would think about the unusual occurrence of the Holy Spirit's coming. Apparently the behavior of the believers at Pentecost warranted a sarcastic remark, accusing them of drunkenness. In reality the Spirit's coming brought power and unrestrained joy. Peter's first thought wasn't focused on whether people liked his message or how eloquently it flowed from his mouth. Rather, the good news of God's activity needed to be shared. Period.

Peter and John later met a disabled beggar seeking financial assistance. The man also needed healing. They spoke words that would have sounded foolish without the subsequent miracle. Yet their concern was not about how they might look if the healing failed. They just spoke to the man in the name of their Jesus and addressed consequences later (see Acts 3:1-8).

Was failure possible? Maybe a better question is to rethink what we mean by failure. Perhaps it's time to examine how this fear of failure keeps us from exploring the journey God has for us.

I continued to learn from the courage of early Christians in the book of Acts. The remarkable saga of the early church was their constant leaning forward to follow God in faith without concerns for personal implications.

For example, when God told Peter to go to the home of Gentiles, Peter said yes (see Acts 10). He dealt with the sticky implications of Jewish-Gentile relationships and religious defilement later as those issues arose in the church. Something freeing exists about joining God on this journey without fearing other people's reactions. More importantly this constant forward-leaning posture of faith resulted in the gospel being unleashed in the first century world.

I've enjoyed reading J. R. R. Tolkien's *Lord of the Rings* trilogy, along with the 150 million others who have purchased the series or the movie version. Likely Tolkien's dark themes grew out of his traumatic experiences in the trenches during the First World War. Tolkien wrote *The Lord of the Rings* in stages, mostly during the equally dark years of the Second World War when evil loomed large to him and his countrymen, and failure in the battle seemed possible.

However Tolkien's writing also developed out of his Christian worldview. He believed "the world is indeed full of peril and in it there are many dark places." Despite all the darkness of ugly and evil characters throughout the books, he offers his readers a sense of hope. He chooses unlikely heroes, simple and seemingly weak creatures called hobbits, writing that, "Even the smallest person can change the course of the future." These hobbits exhibit surprising courage, but they also know fear. The task before these small heroes often overwhelms, as failure seems more than possible; it seems likely.

Will you join the journey? Big issues are at stake involving real people.

The movie adaptation imparts an insightful moment when Frodo, the hobbit charged with the responsibility of bringing victory, struggles. He suffers brutal battles, nearly loses his life and those of his friends. He's clearly overwhelmed with fear, wishing he would have never involved himself with the ring, and desires to return to his placid existence of his now far-away village.

"I can't do this; it's too hard," he laments. His fellow hobbit, Sam, speaks necessary encouragement. "There's some good in this world, Mr. Frodo ... and it's worth fighting for."

The apostles agreed, and it's at this point we must continue the journey. We battle not against flesh and blood, but against spiritual forces of wickedness in high places. Stand firm. Fight the good fight, wrote Paul, leader of the first century apostolic team. Will you join the journey? Big issues are at stake involving real people.

Probably we all wish life could be easier, more comfortable, with fewer risks or fears. We can feel like Frodo in the story, constantly in over our heads, overwhelmed, and even fearing our limited abilities. It's what makes Tolkien's story compelling. His Christ-like figure in the movie, Gandalf, offers wise counsel to those in fear:

> So do all who live to see such times, but it is not for them to decide. All we have to decide is what to do with the time that's been given to us.

God's purposes are worth fighting for and pursuing, even when you're in over your head.

————∞————

"Fear causes a kind of contraction of the heart.
As such it inhibits godly actions such as love,
hospitality, risky mission, and generosity."
      — Michael Frost and Alan Hirsch,
            missiologists and authors

"Christ alone, cornerstone;
weak made strong in the Savior's love,
through the storm, He is Lord, lord of all."
   — "Cornerstone" by Jonas Myrin, Reuben Morgan,
            and Eric Liljero

————∞————

Steps on the Journey

1. What *But what if's* ... have played a part of your story?
2. How do your fears relate to your view of God? Examine each fear in the light of who God is.
3. How have the following thoughts affected your journey with God?
   - What will others think?
   - How am I doing?
   - What if I fail?
4. Spend time speaking to God about these fears.

Speaking to God: *Thank you, Lord, that I have not been given a spirit that makes me a slave again to fear. However, fear remains a reality before me. Thank you for the encouragement of your word, the Bible. Thank you that I walk with others in this temptation. I am glad to know your Spirit lives within me and that His power is beyond any fear I encounter.*

Prayer Log—What is God saying to me?

chapter seven

Relationships
Matter

Three Peruvian friends accompanied me to the airport as our weeks together ended. For an hour, we relived stories of God's activities, sang newly learned songs, and roared with laughter over practical jokes exchanged, most falling on me. On that evening, I didn't care if my flight departed on time, as the delight of our shared friendship overwhelmed me. I thought, *I really love these guys.*

My journey in relationships contained numerous challenges. Living in Chicago and Los Angeles meant the constant presence of masses of people, sometimes numbing me to the individuals living within those throngs. Driving from Los Angeles to rural Iowa for my first pastorate changed how I saw people.

As a twenty-something, I drove a U-Haul truck filled with all my earthly possessions and my expectant wife, Karin, to Iowa. The company motto emblazoned on that rental truck, "Adventure in Moving," should have prepared us; the 2,000-mile adventure went poorly. But we managed to maintain our optimism moving from sunny California to our new Midwestern home — population 1,210.

The first night delivered the biggest adjustment. I think it was the noise … there wasn't any. Instead of the constant drone of hundreds of passing cars and honking horns, we counted three vehicles that passed our house the entire evening. We loved our new home and loved the kind people at our new church.

Our "post-graduate" work in church education progressed well with mostly "passing grades" except that I seemed to find myself repeating the same course each year — Relationships 101. A curious statement I often heard in passing from others proved to be prophetic: "The best things about a small town are the people; the worst things about a small town are the people."

In many ways, that statement extends far beyond small town experience, for life itself involves relationships, accompanied by transcendent joys and deep pains. By design, God has lined our journey with people and relationships every step of the way. Though challenging at times, people really are the best part of the journey. God cares about people, longing to connect relationally with those He loves as well as networking them together for the journey.

Relationships Can Be a Struggle

The biblical prophet Jonah best illustrates the struggle we face in grasping the importance of relationships. His story underscores his reluctance to not only obey God but to connect with people. After God commissions him to preach repentance to the inhabitants of Nineveh, Jonah flees from the presence of the Lord. Talk about relational disinterest!

The prophet planned his getaway from God by boarding a ship going in the opposite direction from Nineveh. A now-famous and terrifying storm developed at sea, requiring every able-bodied person on board to fight to save their lives. As the struggle for survival ensued, Jonah was sleeping in the hull, by himself.

The next three days of Jonah's adventures are recorded as he was thrown into the sea, travelled inside the great fish, and finally was vomited onto land. Throughout the story, Jonah is alone, finally resigned to obey God's call. Reaching his God-appointed destination of Nineveh, the writer portrays Jonah as a solitary prophetic voice preaching judgment.

Expecting rejection, Jonah watched the people embrace his message with repentance. Even though the city's population, from leaders to common citizens, welcomed Jonah's words, the prophet sulked on a hillside a safe distance above the city. Again alone, Jonah hoped against all hope that God would wipe out the repentant nation with a spectacular display of wrath.

But God doesn't destroy anyone in Nineveh, He instead brings deliverance and salvation. At this point, I'd think Jonah could be helpful in discipling these new believers, initiating Bible studies, moving forward with church planting and leadership training. Instead Jonah continues to whine and complain; still he is alone, growing more callous to people who had finally found life in God's forgiveness. Frankly, Jonah looks like a man totally wrapped up in himself. The meager conversation between the prophet and God centered on the weather, a vine-like plant, and Jonah's unhappiness with his discomfort.

In the drama, God adds what seems at first a footnote, though it becomes the main point of the story.

> Should I not be concerned about that great city?
> —Jonah 4:11

That question which closes the prophet's story tells us something about God's heart—that journeys with Him involve people and relationships. The statement and story become a precursor to Jesus' famous words:

> For God so loved the world that He gave His one and only Son, that whoever believes in Him should not perish but have eternal life.
>
> John 3:16

Jonah's narrative does offer a ray of hope. This book of the Bible possesses a confessional feel as Jonah openly shares his failures and relational coldness to the millions who continue to learn from his struggle. Jonah's story in a strange way portrays the gospel.

We're all different in our relational wiring. This chapter may seem unnecessary if you connect naturally with everyone. But perhaps you've noticed few Jonah parallels in your life. Deep down you genuinely care, but connecting with people creates anxiety for you. I didn't write this chapter to fill the world with extroverts, but rather to explore the value of relationships for the journey ahead.

Relationships Can Shake Your Comfort

Baseball legend Lou Gehrig addressed a capacity-packed Yankee Stadium to announce his retirement from the game. His career gave tribute to not only athletic skill, but determination to play through adversity and pain. His record of 2,130 consecutive games played lasted over a half century, but the disease that borrowed his name caused the end of his athletic career and his life at the age of thirty-eight. His famous speech carried words of amazing spirit and optimism. "Today I consider myself the luckiest man on the face of the earth," he said, referring to the relationships that filled his life.

My wife, Karin, and I have often sensed that same favor from God in our relationships. Some began simply enough as ministry projects, as was the case with Patrick, a church bishop in Uganda. Patrick oversaw some 700 leaders and churches in the western part of Uganda — and he appreciated our leadership training model which was especially well-suited to the geographical and spiritual challenges of advancing Islam and cultural animism of his area. As we planned for the training, we became friends, as did our wives. Soon our relationship grew far bigger than the project. We spent time in each other's homes and looked forward to each visit. Karin and I had reason for optimism in Uganda as this dynamic young leader possessed vision and passion.

One day, we received a phone call. Patrick was killed in an auto accident, leaving his young wife and three children behind, a situation virtually guaranteeing poverty and vulnerability. Patrick's sudden death hit me with unexpected force. I felt I had lost a brother; I felt helpless. Because many of us at our church knew him well, we conducted an informal memorial service for him in Colorado. We could hardly believe this tragedy happened. We grieved.

Not long after this event, we received another call. One of our Middle Eastern national leaders allowed a man into his home who expressed interest in becoming a Christian. But this professed curiosity proved to be a ploy and once inside, the man grabbed a screwdriver and attacked our friend. As the two men struggled, my bloodied friend sustained severe head wounds, and was finally rescued by the police. It was a close call.

My friend looked awful. With his swollen face and stitched up wounds, he resembled the boxer Rocky of movie fame after surviving ten rounds. A few days later in a courtroom, he forgave his attacker, testifying that this was only possible because of Jesus. Yet as we rejoiced in what God accomplished, I still struggled with the whole ordeal because this leader is a friend.

Shortly after this attack, I spoke at a church in the same Middle Eastern country. I heard the news but now witnessed for myself what had occurred. Earlier that month, a gunman entered the church grounds yelling, "Convert to Islam or die," opening fire with his weapon. Bullet holes were still visible in the cross.

"Once again," a friend remarked, "the cross bore the punishment we rightly deserved." I was encouraged that no one was killed in the attack and amazed to see the church packed with resilient people. Yet, I agonized, looking into the faces of these people whose stories might have ended more tragically. Years earlier, I would have read this gunman's attack as a mere three-line news story. That day I looked into the faces of people who had become friends on my journey.

Not only do people add to our lives and increase our capacity to love, we find ourselves involved in something far bigger, in a life where we literally become a band of brothers and sisters together.

God weaves these stories of relationships into the curriculum of what He desires to teach us on our journey. Not only do people add to our lives and increase our capacity to love, we find ourselves involved in something far bigger, in a life where we literally become a band of brothers and sisters together. The Apostle Paul's teaching on relationships makes sense, as he spoke about all of us suffering when one member of the body suffers and all rejoicing when another member experiences joy. (1 Corinthians 12:26). We're in this together.

Relationships Can Give Life

My experiences began defining another core value. Biblically I knew that people mattered to God and that somehow people and relationships play a major part of this journey. I started to see what God had in mind as ministry evolved in our church from the *projects* previously described as Project Beyond to *partnerships* in a three-year campaign called Gospel Unleashed. We discovered the "unleashed" language was more than rhetoric; it represented what God was doing through a network of continually expanding relationships. These relationships made a difference.

Kelly is just one example God's activity through relationships. Her initial visit to our church coincided with the launch of Project Beyond. "I was inwardly moved as I heard what God was up to," she said, recalling her feelings in church that day. "I wanted to be a part." Africa caught her interest, and soon Uganda became her passion.

After an initial visit and much prayer, Kelly decided to downsize her job. While this decision meant taking a substantial cut in salary, restructuring her job would provide her with time off during Christmas break and the summer months to travel. Kelly assumed leadership of our initiative in Uganda, touching the lives of many despite setbacks that would have deterred others.

"Jesus does not do things the way we might expect Him to," Kelly said.

Kelly's greatest strength is she loves people! Though present in Uganda only a third of the year, she learned to communicate in the local tribal language and has lived in the villages. When Kelly found a child needing surgery at a school we're a part of, she shared the need, raised the money to help and waited long hours at the child's bedside in the primitive rural Ugandan hospital.

105

Presently twenty young men and women call her Mom. Our work in Uganda has grown under her leadership from one to three mission sites, some in the more unreached areas of the country. I'm amazed whenever I'm in Uganda that everyone knows "Mama Kelly," and they love her. The gospel has literally been unleashed through her.

Recently, Kelly travelled with us to neighboring Kenya though she expressed an atypical reluctance. When I asked about her hesitation, she said, "I'm afraid to go for fear of falling in love with this country too." Sure enough, she did. Her circle of friends grew, as did her love.

"Nothing in my life has remained the same since God called me to serve Him," Kelly says. She feels she is living out a modern-day rendition of the book of Acts, called to serve "the least of these." God's peace has resulted.

When we love someone, we don't run out of love; instead God fills our love reservoir with greater capacity to love.

Kelly's story reminds us of one of the mysteries of relationships. We don't live in a closed universe. By that I mean we're not allotted a limited amount of love, which when used is gone forever. When we love someone, we don't run out of love; instead God fills our love reservoir with greater capacity to love. In reality, compassion in relationships works like a muscle. The more you love people, the more your love grows. As Kelly learned, her capacity for compassion grew. And as her love grew, so did she.

I believe this illustrates Jesus' words in His Sermon on the Mount. He strongly told his followers to avoid limiting the scope of their love to friends and family.

I tell you: Love your enemies and pray for those who persecute you, that you may be sons of your Father in heaven. Matthew 5:44-45

In fact, His closing remarks in that particular section of His message encouraged them to "be perfect therefore as your heavenly Father is perfect" (Matthew 5:48). The context of this impossible-sounding imperative involves expanding the scope of love. He calls us to exercise that muscle of compassion He gave us.

Relationships Can Impact a Culture

During his twenties, Mark travelled to Africa to hunt and to enjoy the adventure of this magical place. He dreamed of returning, but life happened instead. He married, raised a family, became a successful building contractor, and settled into comfortable routines.

Mark sat in church on the weekend we shared the vision of Project Beyond. He could see where it was leading us as a church, but I'm convinced he heard only one word: "Kenya." Thirty years had passed since his visit to Africa. As he listened to an opportunity that existed in Kenya and the need for leaders, the dream came alive again. His wife, Tina, was reluctant to look at Mark; she knew exactly what he was thinking.

Mark's story illustrates how God brings a lifetime of experiences, gifts, and dreams together at just the right time. Our work in Kenya involved children, construction, and Africa—all three were loves in Mark's life. Mark and Tina travelled there to investigate what this would mean. Some details of the plan would change, and the scope of what God had in mind would prove to be bigger than any of us anticipated, but the surprises occurred in relationships.

Mark's friendships, developed thirty years earlier, reignited and soon spread to additional relationships, expanding faster than a day on Facebook. Through conversations, Mark learned of tragic and complicated social problems. These included female genital mutilation, which was commonly practiced in African culture among girls as young at five years old, usually with harmful emotional and physical consequences.

In addition, Mark discovered that these young girls were then typically sold by their fathers into polygamous marriages with older men. Often these marriages took place when the daughter was only eight years of age, and little was being done to prevent it.

As Mark travelled, his concern increased for young girls trapped in these abusive marriages. Our church partnered with an indigenous Christian organization in Kenya who asked if we would be interested in addressing this social issue. That in turn led to relationships with government officials who were eager to see our interest.

Our church purchased property, construction started, and after countless hours of prayer, the Girls' Rescue Center was established. Here, young women are loved, cared for, educated, and equipped with skills to be successful in their communities. Ultimately they transition back into their culture changed by the gospel.

God's power flows frequently through relationships. Soon after travelling to Kenya, Mark sold his business to become our Director of African Development. He allocates much of his year to Africa and then returns telling the story of what God is doing, enlisting support for the work. Tina is a mom to forty young women. And all around the region in Kenya, Mark bears the Maasai name "Saruni, father of the rescued." In my office I have the picture of a rocky, barren field with a simple wooden cross stuck in the ground where dozens prayed. It now serves as the home for the rescued.

Relationships Can Advance the Gospel

Over the years, our church expanded ministries and relationships in Africa, Asia, the Middle East, South America, and at home in Colorado. I became intrigued with a rarely studied portion of the New Testament found in the closing paragraphs of the book of Colossians. You may recall those not-so-inspiring words of final greetings: so and so greets some other guy, say hi for me to the group meeting in another's home, my friends here also say hello, one of our group is working really hard, and did you know Luke the doctor is also here, etc. (Colossians 4:7-18).

These words from the Apostle Paul hardly stirred my soul … until I began to think through the relationships that were mentioned. This theologically oriented New Testament letter suddenly concluded like a love letter listing a dozen people. These *Love flows through relationships, and so does the gospel.* people lived in various cities, some of which Paul never visited, worshipping in churches where Paul wasn't directly involved. In fact, it was all happening as Paul was confined under arrest in Rome, hundreds of miles away.

The light went on inside me. Colossians 4 tells of disciples of Paul's disciples who were unleashing the gospel and making the difference. The passage reveals a legacy of relationships.

I loved this portion of God's Word revealing the vibrant spreading of the gospel through relational connections. Love flows through relationships, and so does the gospel. This transforms the way we think about missional involvement, about the journey God has for us. Mission trips and creating great programs aren't the real point. The journey involves ordinary people willing to go with God and care about people they meet on the journey.

Tracing back those closing greetings in the book of Colossians provides the panoramic wonder of relationships. Paul and his friend Barnabas were once leaders in a church located in Antioch. Under the Spirit's clear leading during a worship experience, the church decided to do something risky. They commissioned two of their five senior leaders to go to unknown parts of the world with the gospel.

What a significant moment in the history of that young church to lose forty percent of its leadership in a single day. There were no guarantees of Paul and Barnabas's return or success, nor would there be any direct personal benefit to the local church in Antioch. In fact, this decision brought relational loss to the church who loved their leaders.

Yet the church followed the Spirit's direction. The work God called them to would not be outsourced. They clearly understood God's heart to unleash the gospel, and what followed was a journey of rich relationships through mostly ordinary people that brought the life-giving story of Jesus to the world. In some ways, relationships are the most satisfying part of the journey.

‒‒‒∞‒‒‒

"We love each other so much in battle. If we see that our cause is just and our kinsmen fight boldly, tears come to our eyes. A sweet joy rises in our hearts, in the feeling of our honest loyalty to each other; and seeing our friend so bravely exposing his body to danger in order to fulfill the commandment of our creator."

— *Jean de Brueil, thirteenth century French knight*

"I no longer call you servants, because a servant does not know his master's business. Instead I have called you friends, for everything that I learned from my Father, I have made know to you."   — *Jesus, John 15:15*

‒‒‒∞‒‒‒

Steps on the Journey

1. Love, when exercised, grows. Do you agree or disagree with the statement?
2. Name the most challenging barriers for you in developing relationships on the journey.
3. God has made you for relationships. Who can you join on the journey?
4. Think of existing or potential relationships in your life. How might the gospel spread through such relationships?

Speaking to God: *Lord, help me understand that I need not be on this journey alone. Expand my capacity to love others. Provide courage for me to take steps in reaching out to people. Allow me to know that in the process you are developing something much bigger than me – a great building, a holy temple in the Lord.*

Prayer Log—What is God saying to me?

chapter eight

You Have
What **It Takes**

Karin and I once stood on top of Mount Nebo in western Jordan. Moses climbed this very mountain at the end of his life. The view captured my imagination. A barren wilderness expands to the east, a vast display of nothing that became home to the ancient Israelis under Moses's leadership. One look at the harsh, grim wilderness and I could understand the people's constant grumbling and complaining.

The area below and to the west holds another story. Your eyes immediately see the large but lifeless waters of the Dead Sea. To the north the Jordan River Valley, marked by a green line of vegetation, brings water and life to the region. Across the Jordan lies Jericho, one of the earth's oldest cities famous for walls that collapsed at the sounds of shouts and trumpets.

My imagination shifted into high gear. As I stood 4,000 feet above the valley below, I thought about Moses, who could see the encampment of his people ready to cross into the land, which God promised them years before. What ran through Moses's mind as his still keen eyesight took it all in and he heard God's voice repeating His promises to give the land to Israel?

Meanwhile down in the valley, Joshua, the new leader, had his hands full. Assuming the mantle of leadership from Moses was daunting, yet God affirmed Joshua's leadership. Even the people's initial response encouraged him. "Whatever you have commanded us we will do, and wherever you send us we will go. Just as we fully obeyed Moses, so we will obey you" (Joshua 1:16-17).

What an impressive expression of commitment by the people! However it wasn't long until Joshua, like Moses before him, faced his own heartaches of rebellion, greed, and defiance from the people. The weakness of the human condition accompanied their words of total obedience and complete availability. If the journey into the Promised Land had taken a couple of hours, all might have been well. Such is not the nature of most journeys.

What will it take to persevere on the journey? Are good intentions sufficient?

One theme of this book traces how ordinary people can create extraordinary impact. God delights in taking people with differing abilities, gifts, and capacities along with Him on the journey, yet we might ask if there are any characteristics common to those on the journey. What will it take to persevere on the journey? Are good intentions sufficient? Are duty and trying harder the answer? God provides a better way.

Think Twice about Going on the Journey

While I love what I do and consider it God's gift to meet people, spend time in places so varied, and see God work in incredible ways, there have been moments that challenged my commitment to continue serving in this way. During our first visit to Africa, Karin and I stayed with Kenyan friends in their home in a tough part of town. Our hosts proved gracious and provided their daughter's room with one saggy twin bed and a mosquito net that clung to us like Saran Wrap. Imagine the hilarious comedy routine we enacted each night as we tried to rest.

We found little food either in local stores or their home. Real life in Africa is just that way, yet we were glad to experience nineteen amazing days there. For the first time in my life I faced genuine hunger without the possibility of meeting that need. No McDonalds or Pizza Hut in sight. However I felt a closeness to Jesus, who also went days without food.

In addition to difficult settings, other aspects of travel can be tough. Separation from my family for weeks at a time can be extremely trying.

Recently one of our church elders and I visited Uganda where a new church-planting venture was underway, focused on coffee growers of the area. Meetings went well; a new church was birthed. Progress in bringing the gospel to a new area was pure joy … well, mostly joy.

We stayed with our national leader and family in his home and found them to be the best hosts. They provided me with the premier room in their home, formerly a chicken coop. I recall lying in bed at 2 a.m. on a night when I knew sleep wasn't going to happen. The "bathroom" was outside, a walk into the thick vegetation of this tropical area. With a hostile-looking dog circling the house all night, I was thinking way too much about that trek.

And then there was the lone mosquito flying around my head, a messenger of Satan sent to keep me awake. Okay, it was only an ordinary mosquito doing what mosquitoes do. In those moments as I kept remembering my family back home and the weeks I was absent, several thoughts persisted. Middle-of-the-night thoughts always challenge me. *What am I doing here? Am*

I making any difference in what I do? How many days until my flight home? I found myself praying something like this: *Jesus, may I go home now?*

Morning finally arrived and brought a new prayer: *Jesus, I'm glad I can do this for you.*

What Makes the Journey Work?

Our journey can resemble the Israelis of past centuries, readily making bold promises to God or to the Joshuas who lead us. We mean well with our words and intentions, but plenty of experiences block our path— some uncomfortable, some that even challenge our decisions to serve Christ.

Our thoughts might urge us to give up and return to easier places, especially when we realize the journey better resembles a marathon than a walk around the block. What sustains us in those moments? I have very good news: we are people of the gospel, and as we have seen, the gospel is good news not only for others but for us as well.

People use the word "passion" frequently, but often with the misunderstanding that passion is innate— either you have it or you don't. I no longer believe that's true.

A personal characteristic sustains us on the journey that enables God to unleash His gospel through us as He intends. I speak of passion.

People use the word "passion" frequently, but often with the misunderstanding that passion is innate—either you have it or you don't. I no longer believe that's true. While some people obviously exude passion wherever they go and others seem unaware it exists, I see passion as something that develops.

All of us know passionate people, as passion is exhibited in a variety of ways. Where I live, people get excited about a particular football team, the Denver Broncos. (At least I think that is the reason for orange and blue hair and painted faces.) I know people who are into golf, climbing mountains, cooking, or politics. We all understand the quality of passion, either personally or by enduring long conversations with others who share their interests.

Christ-like Passion Requires the Gospel

When you think of passion, what comes to your mind? Surprisingly, the word "passion" derives from the idea of suffering. As such, passion refers to what a person suffers or experiences. Yet passion goes beyond emotion to encompass what we feel strongly about, carrying with it an intensity of feeling.

A helpful exercise in understanding passion on a personal level involves writing an obituary about yourself. Hopefully this task will not be needed for some time, however, the project does identify your passions, reflecting what you care about.

Understanding the development of a person's passion can lead to a fascinating insight. We've talked about how the gospel's intent is the transformation of our lives. The gospel concerns far more than refining our theological belief system or making us nicer people or even forgiving sins. Gospel transformation translates into a change of desires and worldview — we're a new creation in Christ, something new and different at a core level.

Think of the implications of this transformation and how the gospel might connect on a heart or passion level. Every part of us needs to be redeemed and changed. As Alan Kraft writes in his book, *Good News for Those Trying Harder*, "The power of the gospel is experienced most deeply by big sinners who need a big Savior." He explains the gospel not as a religious system with

119

new rules to follow, rather the gospel changes us at the very core by what God accomplishes in us. Perhaps the gospel's ability to transform is greater than we thought.

For example, consider this transformation as it relates to our identity, which the Bible speaks clearly about. We have been crucified with Christ and we no longer live, but Christ lives in us. We live this new life through an ongoing trust and faith in Him (Galatians 2:20). Over time, our lives take on more of the characteristics of Jesus who lives in us, including the quality of passion. This great truth calls for some explanation.

Self-styled Transformation is a Trap

One great danger we face involves moving away from this core identity with Christ to thinking of our relationship with God in terms of human accomplishment. New Testament Pharisees excelled in this, which I call *self-styled transformation*. In this approach, we appreciate all that Jesus did for us through His death and resurrection and affirm our belief of who Jesus is and what He has done. We'd likely pass a doctrinal exam. We prayed the prayer; we attend the church services. Sadly, our relationship with Jesus points to these activities, resulting in a gospel about us and what we have done.

Self-styled transformation expresses itself in one of several approaches. We focus on our intellect (what or how much we know), our will (the strength of our discipline and perseverance), or our emotions (spiritual experiences or feelings). For example, intellectually we press to memorize more Bible verses or fill our iPods with great sermons to digest. These rightly encourage and inspire; the danger lies in thinking that how much we know translates into spiritual prestige and growth. I've enjoyed the process of memorizing entire chapters of the Bible, yet question whether my practices generated spiritual growth and change.

Will power is another approach. I personally benefitted from developing spiritual disciplines, yet understand the peril of reliance on my will. The Pharisaical version of this was expressed in the boast, "I am not like other men ... I fast twice a week and give a tenth of all I get" (Luke 18:11-12). We try to be better Christians, vow to pray more, commit to give up bad habits. Our attempts impress but seldom succeed in terms of heart transformation.

Another common approach runs the route of our emotions. In this path, we engage in activity for personal satisfaction. "My life is empty; I need to go on a mission trip or attend a cool conference." This results in feeling good about what we've done. Amazing experiences elevate us to higher, more spiritual levels, but what really changes?

The hazard of self-styled transformation is subtle. We question what harm exists in greater knowledge, intensely emotional high points, or sincere effort. Sadly, the focus of these approaches misdirects us. They trap us in the cycle of seeking the next deep spiritual truth, an even more powerful spiritual experience, or greater resolve to change our lives. Fear or pride waits for us on the other end.

This model of Christian living infected a group of churches in the first century forcing the Apostle Paul to address the issue with great intensity.

> After beginning with the Spirit, are you now trying to attain your goal by human effort?
> Galatians 3:3

Sadly this trying-by-human-effort Christian living has infected us today.

Pastor Alan Kraft continues this discussion in *Good News for Those Trying Harder*.

> For most Christians, the goal of Christ like-ness is thought to be achieved through certain spiritual activities — prayer, Bible study, giving, church attendance ... but do they make us more Christlike? ... When we define spiritual growth as *us* becoming more like Christ, as *us* becoming less and less sinful, what we are actually pursuing is a spiritual path in which we need Jesus less and less.

Self-styled Transformation Produces Tragic Consequences

Here's the problem: Self-styled transformation ultimately robs us of passion, creating disengagement from the journey because it's too absorbed with self and less dependent on Jesus. The Christian life becomes a lifeless production of duty and obligation.

Self-styled transformation ultimately robs us of passion, creating disengagement from the journey because it's too absorbed with self and less dependent on Jesus.

Imagine being in a relationship where you are continually expected to try harder to make the other person happy. What if a relationship is primarily intellectual and focused on passing on information or bullet points about the day's events? Think about relationships dependent on emotional high points or good times. You don't need imagination to see how a relationship will prove empty when two people merely exist and act contingent on the performance of their partner. Disappointment and resentment will build.

By contrast, consider a relationship built on trust and commitment where performance standards aren't required. Karin and I continue to learn how this plays out. We desire to love each other and experience both joys and struggles together, refusing to place expectations or demands on each other. Our days may bring joys or pain with commitment to each other regardless of how the other person performs or tries. There's great freedom in that, even when we fail and fall into old habits. With that freedom comes greater joy and passion in our relationship.

Gospel Transformation Brings Freedom

The alternative to self-styled transformation is *gospel transformation*. Gospel transformation flows from what God accomplishes in us. But this raises the question what does the gospel have to do with passion?

As I write, I've been praying about two specific initiatives that have brought the subject of passion to life. The first involves sending a team into an area of the world historically hostile to Christ. As I visited the area, I dwelt on its dangers rather soberly. However, one of our African friends with me was brimming with a big smile.

"Who wouldn't want to come to a place like this?" he said. "Think what God will do!"

It helped me to see the decision in a more freeing way, through the lens of a different worldview.

The second initiative concerns one of our international partners who lives in an equally dangerous part of the world. He's concerned, with good reason, about the safety of his family, which he temporarily sent back to the U.S. My friend wrestled with the dilemma of whether to stay here or return to the work that might cost his life. His question weighed heavily on me.

"What do you think I should do?" he asked me.

Just a few days later, he boarded his flight to return into the danger.

My friend chose to return for a reason. It's the same reason behind our own decisions to participate on the journey. Jesus once taught that out of the heart, behavior flows (Mark 7:20-23). Jesus understood that instead of tacking on rules or effort, His gospel affects us at a heart level. In a sense we might say passion is God-infused at the very core of who we are.

When we enter a life-giving relationship with Jesus, God plants within us the seeds of a passion for Him and His interests. As we follow Christ on this journey (more on that in a moment), gospel transformation operates at a core heart level, growing and developing that seed. Ezekiel predicted the gospel would create a new heart in us.

> I will give you a new heart and put a new spirit in you; I will remove from you your heart of stone and give you a heart of flesh. And I will put my Spirit in you and move you to follow My decrees.   Ezekiel 36:26-27

Gone is any external self-styled transformation as God implants a new heart in us.

We see God's passion in numerous examples: Jesus' coming into the world, His repeated compassion toward undeserving people, or His insistence to go to the Cross for us. That's passion! As we grow in our relationship with Christ, our love and need for Jesus grows, and passion follows closely behind. Instead of greater effort, our passion grows out of His passion as we walk together on the journey.

It's like a couple who develops a depth of love and intimacy that only can come from years of walking together through all that life brings. That's the truly remarkable surprise about passion; instead of being self-generated, it spills out of the fullness of our relationship with God.

You Can Take a Few Steps Toward Passion

Let's get practical about how this actually happens. God grows passion out of our responsiveness to His leading. Are you open to follow God's promptings? Your own passion will experience growth spurts as you take this action step of desire rather than duty.

In addition, I encourage people to take steps in the journey that may feel uncomfortable. When we're exposed to people in need, whether across the street or across an ocean, it awakens something in us.

God grows passion out of our responsiveness to His leading. Are you open to follow God's promptings?

Years ago, I teamed up with one of our younger team members in a jungle city where we were asked to visit a young lady connected to a local church. As we entered her home, we realized the desperation of her situation. Confined to a bed, she was dying of cancer. Her husband had abandoned her, leaving her with three young children and little strength to care for them. Struggling with the emotion of it all, my teammate tearfully cried out, "We have to fix this!"

Sometimes the fixes aren't there and all we can do is depend on God's Spirit. As painful as those times are, we need those experiences because they allow us to see what Jesus sees even more clearly than we typically do. Passion grows in the process.

One church team returned from India where they assisted partners who ran a facility that helped young women rescued from the brothels of Delhi. As the team shared stories, I felt emotionally nauseated. Maybe it was the image of six-story shacks lining the street for hundreds of yards, all packed with girls and young women forced to service ten to fifteen men each evening. Or hearing that another area offered the same activity only with young boys for sale. Perhaps it was the realization that both occurred in just one city, in one nation, yet the force of it all hit me as so ugly. All sin is sin, but some forms of evil crush me. I felt very uncomfortable.

That day we weren't only exposed to an issue of great need but connected to God's passion. I found myself praying, *God what do you think about this?* Guilt or pressure to act wasn't the issue, nor was I trying to do something to make God happier with me. And believe me, it certainly wasn't about doing something so that I would feel better about myself in light of the suffering of others. When you are a person of the gospel, life experiences produce passion that moves you to action.

Passion grows as we're exposed to pain and willingly take steps toward alleviating that pain. That's the big step. Moving away from the pain is easier and more instinctive; moving toward the pain is necessary. Not only does the gospel produce passion, passion in turn creates action and initiative that's attractive to others. As pastor and author Bill Hybels states, "Sacrifices move people. They melt people. They stop people in their tracks and make them ask, 'Why?'"

At the heart of the matter lies passion.

"Church history is not made by well-financed, well-resourced individuals and institutions. History is made by men and women of faith who have met with the living God."
> *— Steve Addison, spiritual movements researcher and author*

"There is no higher or more ultimate passion than a human being ablaze with a desire for God."
> *— Os Guinness, author*

Steps on the Journey

1. Passion is a characteristic of ordinary people who create extraordinary impact. Rate your present level of passion and commitment in following Christ (10 being white hot; 1 being lukewarm). Where would you like it to be?
2. Try writing an obituary about yourself. What stands out about your life and passions?
3. Read Revelation 3:14-22 through the lens of this discussion on passion. What can you learn from the church in Laodicea?
4. Passion comes from a passionate God. It flows out of the gospel. What steps can you take to develop this gospel pattern of repentance and faith into your life?

Speaking to God: *Lord, I confess that I can grow lukewarm to issues you are passionate about. I desire to grow in my relationship with you on this journey and experience more of your passion. Thank you that passion is not a matter of trying to work something up inside me, but your work in my heart. I look forward to what you will do in me.*

Prayer Log—What is God saying to me?

chapter nine

God, What
Are **You Saying?**

Rachel is a young woman in our church who sincerely prayed, *Lord, I want to serve You,* though she had no idea what that would mean. As a wife and mom who volunteered with the church's children's ministry, she lived in that mystery of God's plan for her life. For four years, her desire for the adventure remained in her heart and mind. Instead of hearing from God, she waited in silence.

Rachel read and prayed, knowing it was easy to settle into the comfortable life and abandon the journey. She felt God had more. One day she read the following Scripture and sensed God communicating personally to her.

> Is not this the kind of fasting I have chosen: to loose the chains of injustice and untie the cords of the yoke, to set the oppressed free and break every yoke? Is it not to share your food with the hungry and to provide the poor wanderer with shelter — when you see the naked, to clothe him and not to turn away from your own flesh and blood? Isaiah 58:6-7

The word "oppressed" tugged at her heart as if God said, "Help those who can't help themselves." Rachel became aware of the plight of women trapped in the horrors of the global sex trade. As a woman, the injustice and pain surrounding this issue troubled her. At the same time, God orchestrated events with the opening of a home in India for women rescued from brothels in Delhi.

The opportunity arose to lead a team to India, and Rachel knew God was speaking to her. From the moment Rachel stepped off the plane, peace swept over her. *This is where I should be.* God had spoken!

Ordinary people have extraordinary impact in part because they're sensitive to God and His leading.

However, understanding supernatural issues like God's work in the world and unraveling God's purposes for our lives can overwhelm us. A sense of mystery will likely always accompany this journey with God, yet with that mystery comes anticipation as we discover God really does desire to communicate with us. Our lives matter to Him.

Ordinary people have extraordinary impact in part because they're sensitive to God and His leading.

In his thoughtful book, *Chasing Daylight*, Christian leader Erwin McManus speaks of a dormant longing for adventure that lies within us. Unfulfilled opportunities dim that longing, but it's not dead. We desire involvement in what matters, and McManus correctly identifies what many of us perceive.

Author Bob Buford also writes of this innate desire we all share to be involved in something significant. The drive for success may dominate our early years, he says in his book *Halftime*, as we strive to complete educations, establish families, build careers, and accumulate the rewards of success. Yet even the achieving of success doesn't satisfy us deep down. We want our lives to matter for something more important, something beyond us. God speaks into the longing.

God Has Already Spoken Through His Son

Before discussing what God is trying to tell us, let's clarify what He's already communicated. The New Testament notes, "He has spoken to us by His son" (Hebrews 1:2). God's communication pathway runs through Jesus and the work He accomplished. Fortunately the Bible clearly describes the reasons Jesus came to Earth. Let's look at that purpose in three ways.

The Son of Man came to seek and to save what was lost.   Luke 19:10

First, Jesus came on a rescue operation desiring to make people right with God. It's not surprising to learn His invitation extended to all kinds of people, whatever their status in life or morality. Jesus taught that all people are lost in their sins and need a savior, and that His death and resurrection rescued people from their separation from God.

The Son of Man did not come to be served, but to serve and to give His life as a ransom for many.
                        Matthew 20:28

Second, Jesus reinforced this purpose of rescue and added that He came to make God known to humanity. Jesus desired for people to understand God's heart. Behind Jesus' words shine numerous examples of His servant heart, from washing the disciples' feet to His willing sacrifice for our sins. Jesus came so that we might know God, with His life and actions declaring,

133

"The Son is the radiance of God's glory and the exact representation of His being" (Hebrews 1:3).

> The reason the Son of God appeared was to destroy the devil's work.　　　　1 John 3:8

A third purpose for Jesus' coming is often overlooked. Jesus purposely overturned what Satan had instigated as people experienced release from demonic oppression, healing, resurrection, and wholeness. Jesus attacked the effects of sin that ravaged people's lives and caused so much pain.

Jesus' purposes connect with what God is trying to say today. They take on a grand theme with broad, worldwide effects, in fact often using a cultural term — the kingdom of God. The idea of a kingdom expands our thinking to realize God has something substantial in mind.

God's Purposes Are Woven Together

Jesus loved people and was concerned for every aspect of their lives. Here's the point. Jesus' purposes did not end with His resurrection. Luke, in his introduction to the book of Acts, wrote that the Gospel accounts describe what Jesus *"began* to do and to teach" (Acts 1:1 italics added). What's clear is that Christ's followers *continued* with His same purpose, evidenced through the pages of the New Testament.

Early Christians extended the work of Jesus throughout the ancient world as tens of thousands were rescued through the gospel. Churches served people in practical, holistic ways. In fact an insightful comment followed the healing of a man by Peter and John as leaders realized though these disciples were unschooled and *ordi-*

nary, they had been with Jesus (Acts 4:13). They showed the same spirit and same recognizable purpose of Jesus.

Cultures clashed with the gospel as it advanced into regions dominated for centuries by Satan. As we would expect, opposition and reaction arose, but Jesus' purposes continued forward

Ordinary early Christ followers grasped their purpose; now they pass the baton to us. How are you doing?

through His followers. The gospel not only released people from their oppression, but initiated cultural change. We see the same scenario played out today when the gospel permeates a culture — the vulnerable find protection, the needy provision, and the lonely acceptance.

The whole theme in the book of Acts reinforces this cultural advancement. Ordinary early Christ followers grasped their purpose; now they pass the baton to us. How are you doing? Do people observe a resemblance to Jesus in your life as they did with Peter and John? Are you living a Jesus-like life? Seeing in a Jesus-like manner? Journeying with a Jesus-like purpose?

We need God's input to see this impact occur; fortunately His help is available. God wants to tell you and me something. Listening to God humbles me because I don't know what's next. In this, we stand alike, dependent on God, listening.

God Desires to Speak to Us

To accomplish His plans, God communicates to His people. Our willingness to listen aids the process, which is illustrated in C. S. Lewis's *The Lion, the Witch and the Wardrobe*. The land of Narnia and its people are under the spell of the wicked White Witch. Under the witch's evil rule, life has grown difficult; eternal winter rules and hope waned. But hope returns with the announcement, "They say Aslan is on the move." Aslan the lion is the Christ figure, the hero who works to rescue and restore.

In the story, the characters who are sensitive and listening understand the message. Perhaps not surprisingly, the heroes in Lewis's drama are four children. Lewis understood that God uses ordinary people to create an extraordinary impact. These ordinary children fought the battles and displayed the courage that ultimately contributed to victory.

In our best moments as a local church, we have listened well and moved toward Jesus' purposes. Hearing from God is embedded in our worldview: we believe God desires to speak to ordinary people and churches to accomplish His awesome plans. His communication has encouraged our congregation to take additional steps on the journey. Here are some specific steps God impressed on us.

Step 1: Relationships

As we studied the Bible and listened to God, we realized relationships matter a great deal to Him. Because God is very inclusive in whom He chooses to love, we pursued friendships with people of various ethnicities, languages, and religions.

Those friendships proved dynamic and even led to some humorous situations. Where else would you expect to be sitting on the ground halfway around the world staring at a meal of camel hump with a nice, warm glass of camel milk? Or trying to be gracious and consume guinea pig grilled on a stick with its cute face still looking at you? Those relational scenes not only make for good stories but have opened the door of God's kingdom. We moved toward people who need Jesus.

Step 2: Availability

Every Christian needs a passport. I have no idea if God's agenda for your life includes international travel, but availability is the point, and a passport makes it possible to go wherever God might lead. A passport communicates your availability, removing many restrictions and limits. More than once I have been astonished to discover where my journey has taken me.

Step 3: Patience

If ever there was an oxymoron, "action steps of patience" sounds worthy of inclusion. How can you be patient, yet take steps of action? However, patience shouldn't be confused with inactivity. I once travelled with one of our leaders to a location that had been at war for decades. While we had differing faiths, this friend and I cared about each other, and he wanted us to help him with projects in his homeland. My mind raced as I lay awake at the end of a busy day. I desperately needed to hear from God as I felt like I was playing a cosmic game of Connect the Dots.

Many connections took root on that trip. Government approval, relationships with tribal leaders, identification of possible projects ... one by one these details came together in an incredible yet confusing way. Our team could see God's hand at work with His favor evident, but we couldn't figure out what the still-forming picture looked like.

Then I uttered a simple prayer. *God, so what are you trying to say?* We wanted some clear direction regarding next steps. I prayed that prayer often and learned in the process that patience is part of the journey. Moving forward, doors opened and eventually a plan developed to bring God's good news to an area of great need. Patient waiting reminds us we need God.

Step 4: Prayer Dialogue

We all know prayer is essential, yet I'd call you to rethink how you pray. Prayer extends beyond a monologue where I talk and tell God what I need to say, and then conclude with "Amen," thus ending any further conversation. Would any relationship mature with such a pattern of communication? Talking and listening are both involved.

I once heard a comedian say, "If we talk to God, that's spiritual; if God talks to us, that's schizophrenia." Many of us can name weird examples of people claiming to hear from God.

But could God want to say something to us? Is it possible to be biblically solid while still sensitive and open to His voice? I firmly believe that is the case. God possesses both listening and speaking skills; He desires to be more than a good listener.

My understanding of prayer includes both speaking and listening to God. Often I pray in response to people's expressed needs; at other times I find myself praying for needs unexpressed to me or taking spontaneous steps of action for no explainable reason.

A couple of years ago, my friend Joe and I spent the afternoon praying with a group of Ugandan pastors and leaders who joined us under a tree in the beautiful mountainous area of western Uganda. We explained that instead of compiling a list of requests and then repeating them to God, we desired to begin by quieting ourselves in prayer. In that stillness we would listen to whatever God might want to say.

"Thanks," one man said as he interrupted me. "But I need your prayer for this pain I have in my side, a sick child at home, money to pay school bills, and a few other very genuine areas of need." As we prayed for him, I felt a strong impression from the Holy Spirit. *Ask him about his father.* Joe had the same impression.

We didn't hear an audible voice, just a phrase that reverberated deep inside both of us. I interrupted the prayer and asked the man, "Would you tell us about your father?" Following a look of amazement, he told us his story. His father was a witch doctor who had cast hateful spells on his son—this Christian pastor—who followed Christ.

I'll let you work through your own theology of what Satan's schemes might look like, but that day brought great release for this Ugandan pastor as we talked and prayed about the oppression he faced and his identity in Christ. God "spoke" to us about something He wanted to address.

While I've experienced God's speaking through an impression, biblical passage, or a mental picture, my purpose is not to be dramatic. Prayer isn't about our experiences as Christ followers, but focused on God, who hears our requests and also speaks to fulfill His purposes.

You Can Hear From God

Great journeys are lined with Christ followers sensitive to the God who leads them. People like Abraham heard God speak. While not given the specifics of what that conversation entailed, we know what he heard was clear enough that he willingly left his people and offered to sacrifice his son, actions he wouldn't seriously consider without certainty that the message came from God.

> *Great journeys are lined with Christ followers sensitive to the God who leads them.*

Moses, Joshua, Gideon, and the prophets all heard instructions from God, so incredible no sane person would naturally pursue them. Yet those godly people listened, and knew with certainty the Lord spoke. Their actions impacted nations.

The first century church learned to listen to God as the gospel was unleashed. For example, Scripture introduces Philip in relatively ordinary terms: the disciples chose him to direct the church's food distribution program. Later God worked through him to bring the gospel to Samaria. At this point, God's communication with Philip grew even more interesting as an angel of the Lord told Philip to leave a significant Samaritan revival and travel on the Jerusalem—Gaza highway. Then the Spirit *told* Philip what specific steps to take when he got there (Acts 8:26-29).

With information and timing only God could arrange, salvation came to an Ethiopian government official who then shared the gospel with a new people group. Whatever the communication looked like, Philip's sensitivity and obedience to God resulted in powerful impact.

Saul heard Jesus' voice on a Damascus road directing him to enter the city. Meanwhile in the city of Damascus, a Christian named Ananias also heard God in a vision, instructing him to go to a particular street address to find Saul. The communication in both cases was clear and specific (Acts 9:5-16).

Peter and Cornelius engaged in similar yet separate conversations with the Lord. Both men talked with God, listened to Him, and then responded. Because they listened, the gospel came to the Gentiles (Acts 10:3-48).

In the same way, the Holy Spirit spoke to the church in Antioch. While they were in worship and prayer, God instructed them to set apart Paul and Barnabas as global ambassadors of the gospel (Acts 13:1-3). Again, their sensitivity to the Spirit's detailed message instigated the catalytic expansion of the gospel.

The book of Acts gives us other examples of God's various forms of communication. The Holy Spirit somehow compelled Paul to go to Jerusalem and also warned him of the hardship that awaited him there (Acts 20:22-23). Then a prophet *[Early] Christ followers didn't think it strange to hear from God.* named Agabus reiterated this particular message, but didn't tell Paul what to do (Acts 21:10-14). Much later, God sent an angel to Paul to provide valuable information during a storm at sea (Acts 27:23-25).

In a passage that has been a source of personal encouragement, Paul's mission team literally wandered throughout Turkey — with God directing them where to go and where not to go. The team needed information; God provided it (Acts 16:6-10).

Based on these biblical examples, what can we learn about listening to God? These biblical accounts read naturally and don't seem contrived or programmed. These Christ followers didn't think it strange to hear from God. In fact, they welcomed the communication, and discovered that listening in prayer furthered God's purposes and plans. Christ followers found listening life changing. God's communication brought encouragement, direction, and hope. Lost people were rescued; God's heart was revealed; Satan's control was broken.

You Can Have Better Hearing

I consider myself a learner when it comes to hearing God, as I wasn't taught how to be sensitive to God's voice. While my own theological boxes included the biblical instances I've already mentioned, I considered those truths past tense, not relevant for today. I don't pretend to possess special gifts in this intercessory realm. Rather as an activist, strategist, and planner, listening to God challenged me. But I'm beginning to get it.

Two passages of Scripture have helped me. First, John 10, when Jesus taught His disciples about their relationship with Him, He introduced the picture of a shepherd and his sheep. Sheep listen for the shepherd's voice. Good shepherds call their sheep by name and lead them. What a powerful and personal element to our relationship with Jesus. He's the shepherd; we're the sheep—the image of care, protection, provision, and communication.

Jesus expands the metaphor: "His sheep follow Him because they know His voice" (John 10:4). The sheep were able to recognize the shepherd's voice while ignoring others'. Familiarity and trust developed between the sheep and their shepherd. The sheep identified the words of their shepherd. Is it possible to become familiar with God's voice and hear from Him?

When my wife calls, I easily identify her voice. Years together have brought familiarity to the sound of her voice for we speak often. Her message and tone have a consistency I recognize well. I know Karin's heart and the kinds of things she would say or request and even how she would communicate those subjects. It gives her voice away every time.

Discerning God's voice is similar. Regularly reading God's Word gives us a familiarity with His heart, His ways, His manner, His purposes. God is consistent in communicating and true to His nature. The Bible forms a foundation in discerning God's voice.

Time also matures our ability to identify God's voice. As God directs you over the years, you become accustomed to how He leads. Patterns of prayer deepen the relationship and allow His voice to grow in clarity. I've noticed that God most often speaks quietly, rarely yelling above all the clutter and noise of our lives. Quietness was a spiritual discipline valued in past centuries; we would do well to give priority to it.

The second passage I found helpful was Romans 8:14: "Those who are led by the Spirit of God are sons of God." The image moves from sheep and shepherd to children and their father. Part of being a responsible parent involves giving direction and instruction to our children. God's sons and daughters are blessed with this expectation as well.

The entire chapter of Romans 8 sheds brilliant light on this family-like relationship. God's Spirit affirms us as His children and prays for us as a parent. The Spirit leads us well. In actuality, Romans 8:14 deepens and personalizes what Jesus taught earlier. We can expect communication with God, including the input of God's Spirit into our lives.

We began the chapter introducing this principle: Ordinary people make an extraordinary impact in part because they are sensitive to God and His leading. That sensitivity deepens through our dialogue with God. Developing the discipline of quietness helps us grow in sensitivity to God, but all of this goes much deeper. There's something life giving in this communication that gives great delight to be led as a son or daughter of our heavenly Father.

Now, we must shed additional light on what God might mean by extraordinary.

———∞———

"Few people arise in the morning as hungry for God as they are for cornflakes or toast and eggs … In many cases, our need to wonder about or be told what God wants in a certain situation is nothing short of a clear indication of how little we are engaged in His work."
— *Dallas Willard, professor and author*

———∞———

Steps on the Journey

1. To what extent are you sensitive to God and His leading as a vital part of the journey? How would you evaluate your reception to what God might say to you?
2. Think through your prayer life. How much talking and how much listening typically take place?
3. Read through the story of Elijah in 1 Kings 19:1-15. Observe how God communicated to Elijah. What did you notice? Are there spaces in your life to hear a quiet whisper from God? What steps can you take to make it happen?

Speaking to God: *Lord, I pray that out of your glorious riches you would strengthen me through your Spirit in my inner being ... and that I may grasp how wide and long and high and deep the love of Christ is. May I be filled to the measure of all the fullness of God. I ask for a growing sensitivity and familiarity with Your voice. In my busyness, I desperately seek times of quietness to listen.*

Prayer Log—What is God saying to me?

chapter ten

The Challenge
of **Movements:**
They Move!

Y ears ago, our church put together a matrix to guide various decisions we faced. These values served as an as important filter of sorts as opportunities and initiatives developed. These values were far from arbitrary, for we wanted our leadership to be biblical and discerning as we prayed and perceived where God was leading us. These values ranged from how we were to live out the gospel to the importance of developing leadership wherever we worked. Occasionally, values emerged that surprised us, such as one that came from Africa.

What stereotypes do you have of missionary life? My earliest image of missionaries included Americans in khaki shorts and pith helmets living in the darkest jungles flanked by tribal warriors with a collection of shrunken heads from well-meaning visitors. And if I was compelled to name a place that fit the stereotype, it was the Congo.

How our church ever arrived in the Congo remains a mystery. It wasn't in our plans, nor did any of our leaders mention it, not even in passing. None of us placed the Congo on our bucket lists ... yet one June day, our team was on its way there. The trip did not disappoint my stereotypes. The road west into the Congo grew increasingly narrow as we approached the border, lined with thick and immensely dark forests. Finally, only two dirt tracks remained as any visible evidence of a highway, created by previous vehicles driving through the grass.

This story began hundreds of miles away. A dynamic African leader named Antony attended one of our church's International Training Institute (ITI) classes. We all loved Antony's heart and eagerness to follow Christ. Our American team returned home as the training concluded, but months later we heard the news that Antony along with another of our African leaders, Alfred, had taken our ITI material to the Congo (DRC). Independently, Antony translated the material into the local Congolese language and gathered fifty-three Congolese pastors to teach what they had learned at the recent ITI. He wanted to develop leaders in this remote area.

What made this initiative especially exciting was that it occurred without outside encouragement, making it thoroughly indigenous in nature. These men simply took what they had learned and shared it with others. For the most part, they did well, though not without incident as a four-day gun battle occurred when rebel forces entered the area. The courageous team made it home and planned to return with more materials and instruction despite the danger. Spontaneous multiplication had occurred.

Are You Good at Multiplication?

This value of multiplication — the process of duplicating disciples, leaders and ministries — began showing up in several places where we worked, accelerating our education in spiritual movements. Others have written with greater expertise on this subject of movements, their characteristics, and history; I just soaked in the excitement of seeing it happen.

We see examples of movements in the book of Acts. As people were added to churches, the number of disciples multiplied, and the gospel extended outward.

Much earlier in my life I memorized 2 Timothy 2:2. "And the things you have heard me say in the presence of many witnesses entrust to reliable men who will also be qualified to teach others." The pattern was simple: Take what you learn and pass it on to others. So Paul taught Timothy who taught reliable people who taught others. This picture was a model of early church expansion and vitality as multiplication took place, and movements began.

Don't misunderstand. God values every single individual. Every life exists in the field of God's vision, and He cares for people by name. But God also delights in movements of people seeking Him. When whole families, tribes, or regions come to faith, it's thrilling to see. And when these groups in turn reach out to neighboring groups with God's good news, it's powerful.

After our experiences in the Congo, our church began to place great importance on spiritual movements. While affirming that every person matters, we desired to see movements of God's Spirit in action, which would in turn affect many for God's glory and the culture's good. It staggers me that we can play a small part of what God orchestrates. Talk about purpose! It doesn't get any better than this.

I must clarify that my role has never been to determine if we're living as part of a movement or not. History is a better indicator of such things.

Stories such as the 1904 Welsh revival where some 100,000 people professed faith in only a few months give us a feel for what God can do, as communities changed, crime plummeted, and justice and kindness swept through cities like a refreshing summer breeze. Today I'm pleased to see evidence of God at work in such powerful ways. It's extraordinary.

There's a New Way to Think About Your Life

Several years ago, Henry Blackaby wrote a best-selling book called *Experiencing God*. Among many helpful insights, he asked this probing question: "What is God doing?" Find out where God is working, he said, then join Him.

Erwin McManus injects an even more helpful question in his book *Chasing Daylight*: "What is God *dreaming*? Is there something that God wants initiated and He's waiting for someone to volunteer?"

This forward-leaning thinking encourages us to consider what God might want us to do. It encourages us to approach life with initiative. Here's the distinction: Do we just wait around for whatever might come, or do we pursue activity we know is on God's heart? The journey adopts a posture of faith and anticipation, then God works with the details that come together as you go. In the process, you become part of God's amazing plans for this world.

What do we really believe? Does God really "so love" the whole world or only people like us?

In some respects, this forces us to re-examine our worldview. What do we really believe? Does God really "so love" the whole world or only people like us? Is He content with the present spiritual makeup of the world as is?

Many years ago, author J. B. Philips wrote a short book with a penetrating title *Your God is Too Small*. In his work, he challenged the thinking of many Christians who had grown content in their relationship with Christ and attempted to push his readers to consider a God who can do anything and desires to do great things.

Isn't this really what we would expect of God? And isn't this what we would hope the nature of the gospel would be? Big. Beyond us. Powerful. Extraordinary! Thankfully God's plans aren't dependent on our capacity or ability, but His.

You Can Pursue the Spirit's Activity

The journey focuses on what God can do. As the Apostle Paul completed his first letter to the Thessalonians, he sent out an appeal to Christ followers: Join in what God is doing. He stressed the importance of living under God's leadership, referencing Christ's return as a major point of discussion and motivation. He then called believers to wake up and respect those who work hard for Jesus. Paul also included a gentle nudge to those idle on the sidelines of the journey (1 Thessalonians 4:13-5:14).

The entire section inspires, with a call to initiative and action, and finally crescendos with a piercing statement: "Do not put out the Spirit's fire" (1Thessalonians 5:19). What interests me is how the Holy Spirit's activity is pictured. The Spirit works like fire.

In Colorado we understand fires well. With plenty of rugged terrain and an abundance of trees, rapidly spreading fires can be an unwelcome and dangerous occurrence. The Holy Spirit works with a completely different purpose; He is benevolent and brings life. Yet the Spirit's work is fire-like in effect.

Jesus predicted He would ascend to heaven and the Holy Spirit would then rest upon believers and empower them as witnesses of Jesus' life and work (see Acts 1:8). His words must have sounded extraordinary to those early disciples, as Jesus said the Spirit's activity would take them from their homes in Jerusalem to an amazing variety of places. Their journey would spread them into their region of Judea, then to geographically near but culturally far Samaria. The ends of the earth, where none of them had ever been, were part of the plan as well. This is what God was dreaming. Soon it became reality.

The activity of the Spirit at work in these ordinary people resembled a fire spreading rapidly in ever-widening circles just as Jesus said it would. Lest we think this big plan was only rhetoric, in reality that fire extended across the world in a remarkably short time. The gospel brought life and hope wherever it went, impacting people groups and nations.

Don't miss the caution in Paul's teaching about the Holy Spirit's work. He implies the possibility of putting out the Spirit's fire, diminishing His effect and expanse. Activity that might quench the Spirit's work makes no more sense than pouring buckets of water on a warming fire. Our intent involves adding more logs on the fire of the Spirit's work. Paul's words to the Thessalonians underline our incredible privilege to cooperate with God's desires.

You Can Plant Seeds That Multiply

Our church sees God's Spirit working on a personal level. We encourage people to join in that activity. We make resources available, something we call "Seed Funds," for people with ministry ideas who are willing to lead them. Seed Funds provide opportunities to birth the dreams God plants in people's hearts, with the hope that it resembles that spreading fire of God's Spirit.

One of the early seed idea recipients was a small circle of women in the church. Becky and Loni were passionate about seeing children in foster care situations loved and cared for. Thus Forever Families began, an organization that links arms with Colorado churches and organizations that long to see every child in our state's social service system adopted by a "forever family." Forever Families provide training and support for families bringing children into their homes and encourages international adoptions as well.

As this developed, people came forward to donate in order to make such adoptions possible. In the eight years of this continuing work, some eighty children now have homes with families within our church. Statewide, the numbers are even greater as Colorado churches worked to adopt nearly seventy-five percent of state supported children. The dream of two women has become reality, and the fire spreads.

Natasha, a young single woman from our church, travelled to Thailand where she met women enslaved by prostitution and grew aware of the global plague of sex trafficking. Returning home, she realized what took place in Asia also occurred in her own country. One day she and a friend, Mandy, visited a local club where the sex industry flourished. That evening, Natasha heard God whisper, *This is where I want you. Let these women know they're loved.*

Natasha's seed idea later blossomed into Love Made Claim, a non-profit organization she founded. She was troubled that the sex industry devalued and objectified women and knew God could give these women the value and identity they needed. Natasha and her team continued to visit the clubs, hanging out in areas where pimps and prostitutes frequented. Instead of lashing out with condemnation, they loved these women and built friendships.

One woman in the industry called Natasha after a visit. The twenty-two-year-old mother of two children wanted out and noticed the genuine care of Natasha's team. She's in the process of getting her diploma and now wants to help other women in the sex industry. The fire grew and spread further.

Seeds Are Available to Plant

Justin and Michelle served as leaders of one of our initiatives. As young parents, they had a concern for couples facing the challenge of raising young children with serious health problems. They befriended hurting couples whose children faced months of hospitalizations and grew to understand the pressures these situations placed on marriages.

As Justin and Michelle dreamed, plans came together for them to start a non-profit organization they called Back to Us. With initial seed funds, they launched their dream of developing a concept they called a "marital Sabbath." They saw the need to bless couples in intense health crises involving their children.

They found couples in pain, weary of lengthy and expensive hospital stays for their babies. One couple's baby spent the first sixteen months of his life in a hospital. Justin and Michelle reached out to care with genuine friendship, lavishing beautiful date nights and getaways for these couples, simple acts of love to replenish their souls. They have helped six families in their first year and found joy not only in this, but in seeing one couple they served work alongside them to help others. The fire continues to spread.

Your life possesses impact far beyond yourself. God loves to multiply.

These stories energize me as they involve people much like you and me. Some in our community acted on passions to teach gang members job skills. Others longed to see refugees integrated into the life of our community. And in a small way each is part of the movement of God's Spirit that none of us wants quenched. Each is like a log placed on the fire that is burning.

Your life possesses impact far beyond yourself. God loves to multiply. And these stories also remind me how secondary geography is in what God does. He can work in faraway Africa or across your street. The nature of the gospel is that it spreads, like fire, through ordinary people.

Small Seeds Grow Big Gardens

When I talk to people who dream about what God can do, I become more convinced the comfortable life remains vastly overrated. While crossing that threshold into the journey is a big step, few if any have regretted the move. We naturally desire complete clarity about our future and how the journey will work out; God instead calls us to trust Him and invites us into the movement of His Spirit at work in the world.

In the responsibilities and routines of our day-to-day lives, we can miss what God is doing. Yet through individuals, churches, and organizations, I believe something extraordinary is indeed taking place.

David Garrison is a mission pioneer, author, and researcher of spiritual movements. His recent book, *A Wind in the House of Islam*, captures another instance of God at work.

In his research Garrison focused on a larger, more global perspective. He defined a movement in terms of 1,000 baptized believers and 100 worshipping fellowships. His findings tell us that in Islam's first thirteen centuries, only one voluntary movement of 1,000 Muslims came to faith in Christ. In the last two decades of the twentieth century, some eight additional movements surfaced. Consider how remarkable that reality is!

However in the first dozen years of the twenty-first century, some additional sixty-four movements of Muslims gave their hearts to Jesus. In his words, "Something is happening, something historic, and something unprecedented." That's God!

God may direct our journey to join Him in a large sweeping movement that affects whole cultures or people groups. He may steer us to impact the life of a young mom, or a refugee struggling to understand a new world, or a little child. It all matters. The invitation God extends to you reads, "Welcome to a new life and the adventure that will make an extraordinary impact."

Throughout history Christ followers have contributed to this greater movement of God. Some became famous; most were unnamed. Their role in the movement differed from those around them—some were given public functions, many worked behind the scenes. Specific ministries varied with their gifts and passions although those details are not the significant part of the story as the Bible states that each of us is "indispensable" (1 Corinthians 12:22).

The question again calls us to what we truly believe. Can this be real? Could God actually be unleashing a movement by His Spirit in the world today? And if that is true, will you choose to be a part?

"In many cases, the 'Sunday-school Jesus' confines Himself only to the changing of men's hearts; the Jesus of the Gospels aimed at changing both human hearts and human society."
— *Vishal Mangalwadi, author*

"Profound encounters with God are important catalysts in the formation of movements for the renewal and expansion of the Christian faith ... Jesus commanded them (the disciples) to go and make disciples of every nation. He did not offer them resources or a plan. He just commanded them to go and promised His presence through the Holy Spirit."
— *Steve Addison, spiritual movements researcher and author*

Steps on the Journey

1. Read 2 Timothy 2:2. Identify the "Pauls," "Timothys" and reliable people on your journey.
2. Consider what God has been doing in your life. What evidence do you see of His activity and preparation for what lies ahead on the journey?
3. As you are praying, consider what God might be dreaming to do through your life. What do you sense?

Speaking to God: *Spirit of God, I long to join in what you're doing in the world today. Instead of quenching the fire of your activity, lead me in how I might contribute to the movement you direct. Never allow me to overlook the individuals you have placed before me, yet help me see and pray for the sweeping movement of transformation across the world.*

Prayer Log—What is God saying to me?

chapter eleven

Let Your Yes
Be Yes

When I think of failed journeys, the most iconic in my opinion was the voyage of the Titanic. This story intrigued me years ago after reading the book *A Night to Remember* and seeing a few movie adaptations of the event. A staggering number of people perished in the icy waters of the Atlantic in April, 1912 as the Titanic sank. Yet behind the tragedy stood a mindset of the people onboard revealing both the cause and results of what occurred.

For our study, the real journey began not in Southampton, England but hundreds of miles west at 11:40 p.m. that night of April 14 when disaster stuck in the form of an iceberg.

For sure, a haze of arrogance lay over the Titanic, which led to a detachment from thinking of what *could* happen. Despite warnings of ice in the area, the great ship throttled at full speed. While designed to carry sixty-four lifeboats, Titanic carried only twenty, far fewer than needed in case of an emergency. A lifeboat drill scheduled for the morning of the fateful day of April 14 was cancelled for unknown reasons. Both owners and passengers onboard had other distractions.

Furthermore they shared a worldview — the Titanic was unsinkable.

As we now know, even after the fateful collision occurred, many of the lifeboats launched were only partially filled condemning other stranded passengers to their deaths. Some people refused to enter lifeboats, not convinced of the danger even after the collision with the massive iceberg. After all, it was said that even God Himself could not sink this ship. Remember, worldview shapes values and behavior.

A second attitude onboard was just as troubling — fear. Sometime after the collision, passengers realized that the Titanic would not remain afloat. But the sinking of the Titanic took time. Specifically more than two and a half hours passed between the collision and sinking, more than enough time to save many of the passengers. Some lifeboats with capacities of forty-seven to sixty-five passengers carried as few as twelve. Despite the cries of people struggling in the waters around them, most of these partially filled lifeboats remained a safe one hundred yards away. Only nine people were taken from the frigid waters; six of them survived.

As Titanic survivor Jack Thayer later lamented, "How could any human being fail to heed those cries?" The answer to his question of course was fear. Those sitting safely in lifeboats feared being overwhelmed by desperate people flailing in the waters, while others thought the suction of the sinking vessel would doom them to their deaths as well. Some lifeboats even extinguished their lanterns so as not to attract nearby swimmers.

The 1997 film version of Titanic contained the most haunting scene of this tragedy. It depicted a lone lifeboat drifting through the waters now filled with bodies, searching for anyone who might yet be living. Upon seeing the bodies of a mother and baby frozen next to them, the officer on board says, "We waited too long."

Today is a Gift

Our journey with God is an adventure in time, using time well. Like lifeboats from the Titanic, waiting can bring consequences. All of us are in different seasons of life. Some walk in early spring-like days of the journey anticipating God's future plans. Or life circumstances or crises may have raised winter-like questions concerning motivation to continue going ahead. Some perhaps settled into life routines with long summer-like days, consumed with responsibilities and challenges, yet believing that God has more for you. Others are further along the time continuum in days of fall, carefully measuring remaining years.

Every season provides fresh opportunities if we can see them. A sense of wonder and curiosity surrounds them, but all are accompanied by caution. The only time we live in is the present. Living in the past is a recipe for tragedy. Dwell on either past glories or regrets, and you miss out on what God is doing right now. For Christ followers, our past is past, forgiven through Jesus' work for us.

Every season provides fresh opportunities if we can see them.

Likewise when we lean into the future and plan, we aren't forced to live in the grips of the *But what ifs...?* and the worries of the unknown that accompany it.

We only live today, with the call to trust God moment by moment. We're fully engaged in the now. Jesus, in a note of irony in Matthew 6:34, spoke that each day has enough to deal with, so why add tomorrow's stuff to your worry list (my paraphrase). This is good news as our future is sure with a God who holds our lives in His hands.

So we seek God today, in the present where we live. Building on the example of Moses and a largely disobedient Israelite nation which missed out on the joy and realization of God's promises, God gives this insight about time: "Therefore God again set a certain day, calling it Today" (Hebrews 4:7). His perspective on time sees today as a gift given to us to make good choices.

What's both fascinating and hopeful about *today* is its freshness and potential. In one of his final messages to his people, Moses spoke of this. Despite their track record of repeated failure and disobedience, Moses set this gift of today before them. "See, I have set before you *today* life and prosperity, death and destruction ... *This day* I call heaven and earth as witnesses against you that I have set before you life and death, blessings and curses. *Now* choose life ." (Deuteronomy 30:15,19 italics added). They were still in the game, still invited to join with God despite their past.

The Gospel Is for Today

It's important to see this living out of the gospel within God's perspective of time. There's a past tense of the gospel as God forgave all of our sins at the cross. God made us right with Himself through Jesus' work on our behalf. Our Heavenly Father has adopted us as sons and daughters. He redeemed, justified, and made us alive in Christ. All this He has lavished on us.

Plus the gospel has a future tense that's equally exciting. We look forward to heaven in the presence of God forever. We anticipate new bodies and long to hear our Savior say, "Well done." We desire to see Jesus reign as king with justice and righteousness in the realm of His kingdom fully realized, and we wait for the time when our present sufferings are swallowed up with the glory that will be revealed in us.

In this book I focus on the present tense of the gospel. Today is a day of opportunity. Now is a time for choices, entrusted to us as gifts. Even as I say this, I'm drawn back to the subject of worldview—how I think about God and my relationship with Him—because talking about opportunity and today carries dangers of its own. Longing to please God, I've walked on that treadmill of performance. I wondered if I am doing enough for God. Should I be working harder to please God, especially in light of the many needs I see? Should I volunteer to take on another responsibility? Have I exhibited enough faith? Do I need to make up for wasted years or poor choices in my past? Can I do more? Give more?

These questions miss the heart of the gospel and serve as pitfalls on our journey. It's not about trying harder or doing more. We live the gospel in the same way we came to Christ in the first place, in repentance and faith. We came in grace; we continue in grace. The gospel takes us from the exhausting rigors of the tread-mill and delivers us into *Today* where we have opportunity to follow God and all He plans for us. Today is where we live.

Don't Wait for Today

A sixty-year-old accountant named Myron joined us on a church-planting adventure in the Andes. I say "adventure" due to the scorpions, tarantulas, and yes, prison experiences we encountered. Again, God worked in tremendous ways. Myron didn't know what to expect, but wanted to see what God might do through him. People came to faith, some were released from addictions, plus new churches were established. Myron participated with the team sharing the gospel. His excitement grew as he discipled new believers and initiated prayer that brought healing to a woman with

165

cancer. More than a mission trip to a different country, Myron journeyed into something far beyond himself — pretty amazing for an accountant.

As we returned home and the team shared about the trip with the congregation, Myron said something powerful. "Don't wait until you're sixty to go on a mission trip!" Since that time, he has participated in the church's work on other continents as well as his own community. "Don't wait." Valuing the gift of time transforms.

God's kingdom work calls out, "Don't wait! Today is the day!"

God's kingdom work calls out, "Don't wait! Today is the day!" All of us choose what to do with this gift of *now*, in whatever season we find ourselves. Because few birthdates of biblical heroes are recorded in Scripture, I find it noteworthy when age is mentioned. Like the twelve disciples, God used Samuel and David at a young age. Yet Abraham's journey with God began at age seventy-five. Moses finally got around to making that decision at eighty. The Bible tells us Enoch began his walk with God *after* the birth of his son Methuselah. Sixty-five at the time, life was just beginning for Enoch.

The Time to Begin Is Now

We tend to look at those advanced ages, thinking they represent the season when life is about over. But instead of focusing on retirement options, these later years possess potential for multiple kingdom opportunities. Sure, fewer years were left for those biblical golden oldies, but they were packed with significance.

Peter quoted the prophet Joel as the Holy Spirit came upon believers at Pentecost. "Your old men will dream dreams. Even on my servants, both men and women" (Acts 2:17-18). Older men and women would dream, and those images would be God-sized. The passage speaks of Christ followers gearing up for significant activities ahead whatever their gender, nationality or age. The Bible speaks of new plans, creative thinking, and God pouring His thoughts and heart into them. God's working knows no limitations of a culture's assumptions about age.

Joe retired after thirty-five years of teaching. His retirement provided time to fan the flame of his passion — teaching, especially matters of the heart. Soon Joe and his wife helped lead what turned out to be "the mother of all marriage conferences." People connected to his teaching; lives were impacted. A new world opened as part of their journey. Today, Joe and his wife, Candy, travel the world investing in people, as they train pastors, pray for needs and provide wise counsel. They continue to dream. As Joe says, "I can't believe we get to do this!"

Are You Still Dreaming?

The late Ray Ortlund was my pastor during some formative years of training. For many years, Ray pastored a large California church we attended. I loved his enthusiasm for life even as he grew older. He shared his prayer, "Lord, don't let me die before I am dead."

His prayer reminds me of a friend named Katie. At age 103, she is more alive than most forty-year-olds I know. She loves the fresh feel of worship at church, exhibiting a positive, never-complaining spirit. And she's part of God's kingdom journey.

When Katie turned ninety, she announced she would no longer be able to accompany me on our mission teams. Traveling had become difficult, but she could sew and quilt beautiful blankets that teams could bring to people in need all over the world. Hundreds of them. As we distributed them, we related Katie's story and dream. "I just want to see the children warm."

At our church, a group of women, of all ages, meet to crochet and knit. Some are confined to wheelchairs. Some are gaining on Moses in age. Some speak only Spanish. Others still raise families. Yet they do great work and pray for every person who will receive their creations. Refugee children in our city wear their hats during colder months. Young girls rescued from tribal abuse wrap themselves in prayer shawls, reminding them that they are loved.

Irv, a semi-retired accountant in his mid-seventies, joined us in Peru. The team watched Irv get on his knees while he taught a group of children surrounding him at a Peruvian elementary school. With warmth and genuineness, he connected with them like a grandfather — and he made an extraordinary impact.

I think Jesus is pleased with the willingness to serve Him. This journey exists for all; it breathes life into a person at any stage of life. Ordinary people of any age can make extraordinary impact … if they don't make excuses.

Watch Those Excuses

An eighty-year-old named Moses settled into the comfortable routine of tending flocks of sheep and goats in the Sinai desert. One day God's voice invaded his complacency from a burning bush. Moses resisted this "invasion" in a way we can appreciate and perhaps identify with. Moses reacted with excuses.

While I can understand being overwhelmed with the challenge of getting into the Pharaoh of Egypt's face to demand the release of his slaves, Moses reminds us how freely excuses flow. *Who am I? Suppose the people ask me a hard question? What if this doesn't work? I'm not a very good speaker. Please get someone else, Lord!* (Exodus chapters 3 and 4).

Excuses. We're each pretty creative when it comes to providing a rationale for non-engagement. We can feel too old or too young. We can tell God we are unqualified or busy, as if He doesn't know. We can even work the spiritual angle, promising to pray about it even when we have no intention of obeying. Or we promise that we'll follow Christ in some specific way, but after some event or circumstance passes. While our role on the journey will certainly vary with home and work responsibilities, it's the way we think about this issue of time and excuses we make that concerns me.

Adopt a Posture of Yes

God invites us on this amazing journey. How do we respond? Minimizing our excuses by leaning toward "yes" is a good habit. When we develop a pattern of responding positively to God, we entrust the details of the journey in the hands of One who loves us and understands our circumstances.

> *Minimizing our excuses by leaning toward "yes" is a good habit.*

He knows our strengths and limitations. He's a good God we can trust.

Our Spanish-speaking congregation participates in our Project Beyond story. They help us plant churches in Peru, and leaders from our partner churches in Peru live in the United States to help us plant churches here. Consequently, numerous people have come to faith along with new leaders trained and an increasing desire to establish other Spanish-speaking churches.

I love participating in the baptism services for the people who have found Christ through the ministry of our local Spanish congregation. Their stories of Christ's work and the excitement of new faith continue to rejuvenate my soul. Our Spanish congregations adopted a Peruvian custom of sharing testimonies of faith followed by singing *"He Decidido Seguir a Cristi"* (I Have Decided to Follow Jesus) as each person is baptized. The last line of the chorus reinforces the depth of their commitment: "No turning back, no turning back." It speaks to the posture of yes.

I greatly respect my friend, Doug, who experienced a painful season in his life. During that time, I sensed I should ask him to join us in Peru. Even as I asked, I realized he could say no for many very good reasons.

Doug soon boarded the plane with the rest of us. It became clear Doug was created for this. Despite having no Spanish language skills at the time, he connected with everybody. At the end of our trip, a person or two typically goes to the airport to say goodbye to each team member. Doug had an entourage! In ten days, something extraordinary happened between Doug and the people.

When he returned home, he began reading books on how to speak Spanish, and soon he spoke fluently. He's visited Peru several dozen times, both on his own and more frequently leading teams from our church. His is a story of extraordinary impact where many people now follow Christ because of his simple yes response to Jesus.

Doug now leads our Peru initiative. His impact expands, as he's instrumental assisting other people and churches. As an aside, God worked through these trips to provide Doug with a wonderful wife.

Something extraordinary happens as we say yes. Businessmen and women use their gifts to further kingdom work in sustainable projects. Intercessors pray to great effect. Young children give their shoes so children in Uganda can wear their first pair, which prevents infections and parasites. An excited young girl once stopped me on a Sunday and asked, "Do you know that I bought a goat for the Rescue Center in Kenya?" That means fresh milk and nutrition in a place where malnutrition is common.

The sinking of the Titanic was tragic. What could have been if passengers had viewed their final hours differently ... if they had seen the opportunity to save lives ... if they had filled lifeboats and moved past fears to rescue those still alive ... if they had rallied past excuses to say yes ... and if they had not waited too long.

What about us? Someone said when you stop learning, you start dying. The opposite impacts us even more powerfully. The journey's experiences as we walk with God make us alive! Multiple entry points connect to the journey, but all begin with the simple word yes. But let's not wait too long.

------❈❈❈------

"Yesterday is history, tomorrow is mystery, today is a gift. And that's why they call it the present."
— *Mike Ditka, former football player and coach*

"Choose for yourselves this day whom you will serve ... But as for me and my household, we will serve the Lord."
— *Joshua, in Joshua 24:15*

------❈❈❈------

Steps on the Journey

1. Someone said choices are the most spiritual activities you can have. What choices await you today as you think about your journey?
2. Give God thanks as you recall what He orchestrated in your past. Give Him praise for the future He is preparing for you. Spend time offering yourself to God this day.
3. Excuses come naturally. What excuses do you offer to God to delay or reject what He desires for you?
4. Each of us is at a different life stage. What do you sense God has for you as you live for Him in the present?

Speaking to God: *God, help me to understand the mystery of time. Show me the importance of living not in the past or the future, but today. I desire to make choices today that will further your work as I journey with you. To You, I offer my yes.*

Prayer Log—What is God saying to me?

Getting
Started

I played basketball in my younger days. Sometimes I started; sometimes I came in off the bench. On our team, we had to be ready to play at the coach's call, and we had to be flexible to fit whatever role or position he needed. I discovered those traits — flexibility and readiness — are necessary attributes for those who desire the gospel unleashed.

Flexibility and readiness call for more than adjustments to new cultures, with new foods, new communication, and new living situations. They go beyond the long hours of work we put in each day with schedules that can border on stressful or occasionally cross that border into the land of crazy.

I speak of leaving our agenda and rigidity about how events, people, and experiences ought to go to open ourselves before God and desire whatever He might have for us.

Are You Ready to Begin?

It's easier for God to lead the flexible person who doesn't demand or set parameters around what life should bring. I realize Jonah was an exception of how

God can lead even the most rigid of people; however I'm sure few of us would want the route it took Jonah to get to the place of God's intention.

We need flexibility because we just don't know the significance of what lies ahead. God may have planned a life-defining moment for you. He may want to teach, direct, or transform you in some particular way. He may take you far beyond what you expected or even dreamed. Are you ready? Often that moment is disguised. Are you flexible enough to say yes?

Your Actions Speak Louder than Words

David of biblical fame faced such a moment which became the biggest day of his life. Before he ruled as king and lived in a palace, David was unknown, very young, and ordinary. His brothers perceived him as an annoyance. But this one day changed his life forever. It set his future on a new trajectory that led to extraordinary impact. I call this time Day 41 for reasons we'll see in a moment.

David was the youngest of eight boys in the family of Jesse. They raised sheep in the Bethlehem area, and David's lot in life was to tend to his father's sheep, among the most common and routine jobs of those days. His nation of Israel was once again at war against their nemeses, the Philistines, who lived nearby in present-day Gaza, precipitating ongoing raids and battles with the people of Israel. As Day forty-one approached, the battle advanced within twenty miles of Bethlehem.

Some of David's brothers fought in the army which concerned his parents. Jesse sent young David to the battlefront with a lunch pail of food for the brothers and hopes of hearing how both his sons and the battle progressed. It was a humbling task for David.

When David arrived, he saw something that stunned him and should amaze us as well. The scene revealed what had become of Israel, exposing their worldview and how they saw God and themselves. David discovered the two armies lined up on opposite sides of a valley. A challenge came from the Philistines to send out a representative to fight one on one. Whichever combatant prevailed determined the outcome of the war and who would serve who. This went on for forty days without a single Israelite volunteer.

David wasn't troubled that the Philistines sent out Goliath, an enormously powerful and intimidating figure. He was troubled that Israel sent out no one! For sure, fighting this warrior carried high risk, but David could hardly believe no one would face the giant. The entire army was immobilized, cowering in fear before Goliath (1 Samuel 17:24). This scene was reenacted not once, but twice daily over the course of forty days. Nearly six weeks of humiliation and ancient "trash talking" assaulted the demoralized Israelite army. And their king, Saul, hid in his tent and did nothing.

Israel's worldview stood uncovered. The Israelites did nothing because deep down they believed God was not big enough or caring enough to help them. Genuinely believing they were in a hopeless situation against a stronger foe, they retreated in fear. Whoever faced Goliath would be carried back a dead man. The army believed this and responded accordingly.

By contrast, consider David's core beliefs.

"Who is this uncircumcised Philistine that he should defy the armies of the living God?" he shouted in disgust (1 Samuel 17:26). Not only could David do some trash talking of his own, he truly believed even the giant Goliath was no match for people fighting for the living God. He really believed it, enough to put his own life at risk. He reminded the king that the Lord had already delivered David from a lion and bear. He *knew* God would do the same against this foe.

We all know the rest of the story. David saw victory as he approached the Philistine. He announced what he believed as true. "The battle is the Lord's" (1 Samuel 17:47). With only a sling and five stones, the battle lasted but minutes. And life changed for David ... on Day 41.

You Can Take the First Step

First steps are significant because we act on what we believe. Even in facing significant obstacles and intimidating situations with limited abilities and resources, David's steps of faith mattered. In that moment, David's actions caused a shift in the thinking of an army. In a plot twist, the Philistines suddenly ran in fear. Hope and optimism overflowed from David to empower demoralized soldiers; joy returned to Israel and those present learned it's the Lord who saves, not swords, spears or bulging muscles.

We too must come to grips with what we believe about who we are and who our God is.

As we fast forward 3,000 years, we must realize life hasn't really changed. For sure, different giants appear but they're accompanied by the same fears. The context of our comfortable situations may look different from the sleepy hillside of an ordinary shepherd with his sheep, but we must also decide if we're ready to follow God's call. We too must come to grips with what we believe about who we are and who our God is. That leads to the same passion David possessed for the honor of God and his cause. God still speaks and still moves; extraordinary impact results.

You're More Needed than You Think

The subjects we've discussed in this book are important. The gospel possesses a natural missional trajectory to it. Your journey with God delivers not only personal transformation but tremendous benefit to others.

In his bestseller *The Tipping Point*, Malcolm Gladwell makes the case that ideas and messages spread much like viruses. He challenges our default thinking that change must take a long time and only comes in steady but small increments. As a result, we expect little impact from our lives. But Gladwell unmasks the fallacy of our assumptions noting that change can reach epidemic levels quickly. One child with a virus easily infects an entire classroom. The HIV pandemic, for example, exploded globally with amazing speed. Personal and societal transformation work are much the same. If sociology affirms this, think about how transformation works when God gets involved.

Understanding the power of the gospel should encourage us. A powerful phenomenon occurs when relatively small numbers of Christ followers think and behave differently. Change ripples outward from a few people transformed by the gospel, reaching a critical mass or tipping point, and widespread transformation emerges. What began small turned into something very large. The gospel was unleashed, as God designed it to be. What Gladwell termed the "Law of the Few," the Bible calls a work of the Spirit.

What is Your Dream?

After visiting India, I couldn't erase the image of hundreds of young girls trapped in sleazy apartments, each dressed up to attract the horde of young men out on the town in search for the cheap thrills of sex. The daily lives of these girls consist of serving sexual appetites nightly for the benefit of those who keep them enslaved. What possible answer is there to this societal nightmare?

The answer lies in the gospel. But what does the gospel look like in such a dark setting? A church in India led by its pastor Sanjiv spawned multiple dynamic ministries that reached into nearby brothels. They decided to live out the gospel in the context of one of the planet's horrific curses, sex trafficking.

Young women from the church opened an office of their own in the center of the prostitution district, meeting with young women and their madams. The church families welcomed into their homes the children born to those prostituted against their wills, in hopes of breaking the cycle.

They initiated schools in communities consisting of nothing more than cardboard shacks amid small mountains of garbage and debris, the only Christian presence in those neighborhoods. They've opened their homes to girls rescued from the brothels and provided a place for girls to live where the love of Christ shines. They've developed curriculum on gender awareness which they present in schools in hopes of turning the tide.

Does it sound like a mega-church of thousands? Perhaps, but these eighty people living in a religiously hostile setting are living out this "Law of the Few." We need not wait for the majority to get on board. A tipping point can occur early with passionate people empowered by God.

A relative few in Africa, people like Larry, Deb, and Jacob have spread the "virus" of the gospel to several African nations through an amazing indigenous network involving hundreds of African leaders. Their leaders carry vital training to several nations in the form of sustainable agricultural, literacy, and medical projects.

Other emerging young Africans like Alfred and Antony fearlessly impact many hundreds of lives. People with limited resources but unlimited passion, like Juvenal, Katty, Benjamin, and Anita, pioneer new works and churches in countries throughout South America. Plus through only a relative

Radical change is very possible. That's the nature of the gospel and our heritage as Christ followers.

few followers of Christ, many embrace Jesus in the Middle East. In one city, a few dozen Middle Eastern believers visit 150 Syrian refugee families weekly to care for their needs and launch Bible studies.

That's how the gospel works, with ordinary people!

Radical change is very possible. That's the nature of the gospel and our heritage as Christ followers. Such action is desperately needed, but like David, somebody has to challenge the prevailing worldview to go for it. Somebody has to take a few steps out toward the giant.

Just Do the Right Thing

Like the river flowing toward the awesome and beneficial power of Niagara Falls, God desires to work in you. Out of you will come streams of living water which will flow to your family and neighbors, and then through your church. God in you can bring living water to your community and even the world. None of us knows where this river ultimately takes us, but that's God's part of the story. Yours is to begin … and embrace the journey.

Like David, perhaps you start with lions and bears and go from there, seeing what God can do. It might mean exploring that next mission opportunity, visiting a refugee family in your own community to help in practical ways, gathering a few others to pray bold prayers together, or talking to your pastor. Here's the question: What does God want to change about your life? That's where it begins. Day 41 is here.

None of the people I've mentioned in this book had lofty expectations or grandiose aspirations for greatness other than a simple desire to follow Christ. What they did just seemed like the right thing to do, reasonable in light of what they knew about God and His heart.

[Bonhoeffer and von Dohnanyi] saw nothing heroic in their actions but instead believed they had simply taken the path a decent person inevitably takes.

David felt this way. He didn't enter the arena thinking victory against Goliath would make him a famous king and beloved biblical figure for centuries to come. He acted in order to honor the name and purposes of God.

In their book *No Ordinary Men,* Holocaust researchers Elizabeth Sifton and Fritz Stern record an interesting account of the days of Nazi Germany. They tell their story through the eyes of a German pastor, Dietrich Bonhoeffer, and his brother-in-law, lawyer Hans von Dohnanyi. These men resisted Hitler's Nazi agenda and supported the rescue of Jews who would have otherwise been taken to death camps. Both were discovered and hanged for their resistance just a month before the war's end and are now often celebrated as martyrs in this cause.

What's most interesting in the authors' retelling of the story was how Bonhoeffer and von Dohnanyi never allowed themselves to speak of their actions in language of possible martyrdom. They saw nothing heroic in their actions but instead believed they had simply taken the path a decent person inevitably takes.

This remains the premise of this book. Our calling to the journey God has for us is simply the path Christ followers take. It's not about glory or personal advance; it's about Jesus. What distracts you from the journey?

I believe there's a desire deep within longing to be awakened. Does your heart cry for transformation, to live a life that somehow makes a difference? There's a way to get there, a safari or journey God directs.

All of us are positioned at various places upstream on our metaphoric Niagara River. And from our present vantage point, there's limited awareness of the spectacular power of God that will be unleashed ahead. We may be unaware of the benefit that will come to so many. It's all mist from here, and that's fine.

In his classic work *The Weight of Glory*, C. S. Lewis summarizes the life journey God's people travel. He speaks of the wonder of God's ways and the power of His working. And he says what I think we all realize deep down in our hearts. "There are no ordinary people." All of this awaits you.

The Bible paints a picture that helps me on the journey. Though set in the future, it's not difficult to imagine.

> After this I looked and there before me was a great multitude that no one could count, from every nation, tribe, people, and language, standing before the throne [of God] and in front of the Lamb [Jesus]. They were wearing white robes and were holding palm branches in their hands. And they cried out in a loud voice:
>
> Salvation belongs to our God, who sits on the throne, and to the Lamb.   Revelation 7:8-10

I'm moved when I think about this future scene of multitudes around God's throne, giving Him praise along with angels and believers of the ages. I try to imagine the stories that will be shared — stories of risks, steps of courage, overcoming fears, and passion. They'll speak of transformation through the gospel and adjustments in worldview. They'll tell of the moments when God spoke, and they followed.

All will stand there because of Christ, for sure, but in part some will be there because of you. Faces may catch our eyes on that day, faces of Abraham and Sarah, Moses and Joshua, David and the Apostles. But most will be the faces of otherwise ordinary men and women who braved the journey.

And yes, Jesus will be there making it a happy day. The movement of God's Spirit did occur. With a force greater than Niagara, God's power was unleashed … in you!

"Until justice rolls down like waters, And righteousness like a mighty stream."
— Martin Luther King Jr.,
pastor and civil rights leader

No guilt in life, no fear in death
This is the power of Christ in me
From life's first cry to final breath
Jesus commands my destiny
No power of hell, no scheme of man
Can ever pluck me from His hand
'Til He returns or calls me home
Here in the power of Christ I'll stand
— "In Christ Alone"
by Keith Getty and Stuart Townend

Steps on the Journey

1. Flexibility. Readiness. How would you describe your default approach to life in relation to these traits?
2. The account of David and Goliath reveals so much about worldview and why people respond as they do. Summarize your own worldview. How do you see God? His purposes? Yourself?
3. As you process what you have read, what might be your next step as you consider God's leading?

Speaking to God: *Lord, I am ready to be a part of the journey you have for me. You have already prepped me for what's ahead. You have promised your presence as I proceed. Thank you for this privilege of journeying with you. And thank you for this gift of today. Let's go. Amen.*

Prayer Log—What is God saying to me?

Vision and Execution: A Word for Pastors and Leaders

"God is able to do immeasurably more than all we ask or imagine, according to His power that is work within us" (Ephesians 3:20).

Josh and Carrie noticed the growing refugee population in our city, meeting needs as their schedules allowed. Though busy working and raising three young children, they possessed unleashed hearts that directed them toward the hundreds of local Karenni refugees. Each Sunday, they filled their two vehicles with refugee families as they drove to church.

The only man numbered among these guests was Soe Rey; he spoke no English. Can you imagine what raced through his mind entering a building called church, hearing a strange language, meeting people gesturing greetings, and watching his children race somewhere with other children to activities designed for them? Strangely, he loved it.

Josh and Carrie prayed for Soe Rey and his family, and one day something totally unexpected occurred. Though he'd never experienced anything like it, Josh saw a clear mental picture of baptizing Soe Rey, who smiled as he came out of the water.

Then the unimaginable unfolded as Soe Rey invited Josh and Carrie to his home. The couple arrived to find the extended family gathered. Through an interpreter, Josh said, "Has anyone here ever heard about Jesus?" Before the evening ended, many embraced Christ as Savior and Lord!

This group formed the nucleus of a new church. A young lady, Say Me, served as the translator and soon followed Jesus, even changing her name to capture her new life. On Easter Sunday, Josh and Carrie baptized Soe Rey and Say Me in a scene reminiscent of the vision received three years prior.

"It doesn't get any better than this!" Josh exclaimed.

My ministry years include both lead pastor and staff roles. I understand that personal transformation is one thing; changing churches can resemble steering the Titanic through a sea of icebergs. I believe there's hope for our churches and that the information in this book directed to individual Christ followers can prove applicable to churches as well. Individuals experiencing God's transformation infect others within your congregation, bringing health and vitality.

Josh and Carrie's story raises our hopes as leaders. Their unleashed journey impacted their Jerusalem, yet touched Earth's uttermost part as Jesus intended. Could such a movement of God's Spirit create new patterns and passions in our churches? We'd all welcome such a possibility.

My mind is filled with such dreams for God's church. Unfortunately, I also see a structural barrier to unleashing the gospel through our churches.

Unleashed Churches Have an Organizational Side

Churches are more than organizations as we know; they're living organisms in which the Holy Spirit lives. Yet, the church is described organizationally as a complex body with diverse parts all working under the coordination or leadership of its head. Each member has necessary functions and importance (see 1 Corinthians 12).

I saw incredibly gifted members of the Body come to life when allowed to function as they were designed. As my journey involved managing numerous global and local projects, I quickly understood failure loomed if everything happened through one person or small leadership group. Too much occurred in too many places to sustain … unless we revisited our structure.

God entrusted people with His gospel. Do our churches follow a similar pattern?

Top-heavy organization limits impact. Such control wears out pastors, frustrates congregations, and over time creates a culture of passivity where a congregation observes its pastor and a few doing the work. We instinctively know more functioning members increase the health of a church. Jesus modeled this by commissioning first twelve, then seventy-two others into ministry.

In the book of Acts, the Holy Spirit continued this model, directing Christ followers into the world. Stephen, Barnabas, Philip, Silas, and Timothy were mentioned with many more remaining anonymous. In each situation, God entrusted people with His gospel. Do our churches follow a similar pattern?

At our church, we operate in a ministry model where a gifted management team oversees initiative leaders who in turn lead the specific projects, preferably in teams. Strong leadership, combined with ministry responsibilities spread among many, help accomplish what God has set before us.

Ministry is Meant to be Shared

Karin and I enjoy presidential libraries. The history and creative displays chronicling recent presidencies is amazing. Beyond their interesting artifacts, these high-capacity leaders provide instruction — especially one surprising president, Herbert Hoover.

Admittedly, Hoover never ranked with the great presidents. He's usually connected to a historic stock market crash and Depression which devastated our nation in the 1930s. His four years in the presidential office weren't his shining moment. Something else captured my attention.

I learned Herbert Hoover's grasp of structure. After each of the world wars, he organized massive humanitarian efforts as the wars left chaos and millions of starving and homeless people across Europe. After World War I, for example, Hoover persuaded thirty-two nations to work together to save 220 million people from acute famine. Despite significant political and logistical hurdles, Hoover and his program succeeded.

The situation proved more grim in the post-World War II aftermath. Hoover organized fifty nations to feed and clothe a third of the earth's population, many of whom would have died without this assistance.

I searched for clues to how Hoover did it. There had to be a leadership principle buried in these monumental efforts. I found it in Hoover's axiom: Centralize the vision, decentralize the execution.

The statement seemed brilliant. As leaders, we cast vision and chart out the direction, while others are entrusted to make it work. This carries risk as expressed by one initiative leader, "So do you actually trust me with this budget and initiative to do this ministry?" My answer was, "Yes, that's the way it works."

This model of leadership played out well as leaders led with skill. Business author Jim Collins articulated it as getting the right people in the right seats on the bus. Jesus led in this way—imparting vision and empowering disciples for the work. The New Testament model explicitly gives leaders responsibility to prepare God's people for works of service (see Ephesians 4:11-16).

Dudley, a missionary for years in Eastern Europe, lives out this principle in leadership. We became friends as events led him back to our Colorado church. Dudley is a fantastic teacher, engaging students in the Word of God. As the vision to invest heavily in training international leaders took shape, one thing was clear—we must entrust Dudley in this work.

Dudley now oversees international leadership development where hundreds of global leaders benefit and grow through his teaching teams. Expansion exploded. It would have imploded had we missed this model of leadership and Dudley's passion.

You Can Overcome Fears in Leading

I hear your questions. "Is there a downside to this structure?" "Will ministry grow out of control?"

Decentralizing ministry can be scary business demanding care in selecting leaders. Yet wasn't this the same issue Jesus faced? We enter leadership decisions prayerfully and with the input of others. And yes, there is great value in building in controls especially whenever finances are involved.

Honestly, I feel this leadership principle attacks our security as senior leaders. It forced me to examine my own leadership style. Did I need to be at every table, giving approval at every step of every initiative? Could

I let jointly approved budgets work, giving freedom to others to lead as God might direct them or even as they made mistakes? Was I really the ultimate expert and guru of all things or has God gifted others in areas where I'm weak? The questions had obvious answers.

Relinquishing control was scary, yet when you have trustworthy leaders, ministry advances. You can focus on responsibilities God has placed before you; so can the leaders you work with.

I identify with the challenges you face as a Christian leader. Sometimes, leading is hard. Wear and tear accompany ministry, as we witness evil and fight the good fight.

Leaders grow weary. We need rest and those disciplines that bring refreshment. Someone stated that when he goes to heaven, he wants to go tired, using the energy God entrusted to them. Sometimes that's part of the journey; however we must not go it alone, discipling others to share the ministry.

My experiences—over fifty trips to the Middle East, Africa, Asia, and South America plus decades of ministry in my community have served to reinforce my developing worldview. Regardless of how things first appear, God accomplishes His purposes and delights in our persevering faith. And He delights to see us enlist and mobilize others for the work. Be encouraged.

Take bold steps in your leadership. People need a Nehemiah to present the vision God has for them as the church.

Take bold steps in your leadership. People need a Nehemiah to present the vision God has for them as the church. Yet give people a structure that allows them to function with their gifts and passions. Stir people to dream; help them flourish in God's design. Grant freedom to pursue the journey and grace in failure. That's courageous leading. The whole church wins.

A plaque on my wall reads, "From small beginnings come great things." Referring to a mustard seed, Jesus reminds us of this way of the kingdom, regardless of the size or location of your church or your personal abilities. These details matter little; your leadership matters much.

⟨∞⟩

"For we are God's workmanship, created in Christ Jesus to do good works, which God prepared in advance for us to do."

— Ephesians 2:10

"The church was never intended to be a monolith but a movement creating moments that change history. . . It radically impacted culture."

— Erwin McManus, Pastor and Author

"God is at work 24/7, all over the world, filling His followers with grace and mercy and power to reclaim and fix this broken planet."

— Bill Hybels, Pastor and Author

⟨∞⟩

Steps on the Journey

1. What are the stated goals of your church or organization? How would you express your church's vision?
2. Evaluate your leadership structure. How has centralization/decentralization worked out for you? Do you desire any changes?
3. Read Ephesians 4:11-16. Moving ahead, how do you perceive your role as a leader?
4. As you pray for your church and leadership, what next steps come to mind?

Speaking to God: *Lord, I know you are able to do immeasurably more than I can ask or even imagine. I also know your power is at work in the church. Help me to see what You see. Provide courage in all you call me to do. And give favor as we move ahead on the journey. Amen.*

Prayer Log—What is God saying to me?